Sculpting Rough Ideas into Elegant Business Plans:

Ideas to Action or Building a Successful Business Plan-Venture Capital-Ready in 8 weeks

Dr. Helen Eckmann
Kerstin Young, BBA & MBA

Printed in the United States of America.

ISBN: 978-0-9982916-8-0

This book offers encouragement and insights to all who have business ideas but might lack the confidence and/or experience to sculpt those rough ideas into elegant and successful business plans. People are often under the misconception that someone needs to already be successful and an entrepreneur to write a business plan. In reality many successful businesses have been imagined, shaped, and run by people who had to read, learn, research, and become experts in diverse fields even though they did not have formal business experience (great examples are Musk, Gates, and Balmer).

In addition, this book offers a guide based upon academic and professional key insights on strategies for writing a business plan. The traditional business plan that have twelve sections and is preferred by many funding sources is presented herein in detail. Those who do or do not have business degrees can become successful business plan developers by reading and following the steps provided here. A great array of business plan outlines and templates are available for download online (and sources are given in this book).

However, additionally, this book offers the necessary steps to take a spark of an idea to a fully developed and successful business. Reading and following concepts offered provides a broad scope and deep understanding of all of the business elements, like innovation and strategy. These often theoretical business concepts come to life with visualized and actual examples and systematic applications of how business works. This book will ultimately prepare anyone with a great idea to become a confident entrepreneur who can present his or her business plan to funding sources.

This book prepares three target audiences to write a successful business plan: Students, innovators, and entrepreneurs:

1. Students who are to become entrepreneurs through building a business plan as a capstone project
2. Innovators who have fantastic business ideas but fear that they might not have the business savvy to build a relevant and detailed business plan
3. Entrepreneurs who have great ideas and want to build a business plan suitable to gain respect (and funding)

The book introduces systematic processes to successfully apply leadership and strategy. Students inside a classroom setting, those who consider themselves lifelong learners, innovators, and those who are likely to start a business, will discover simple and clear explanations of the "pre-work" necessary to sculpting a business: the business plan. The book takes "Ideas to Action" and assists "a good idea" to become a vibrant and viable business. The necessary processes have detailed explanations with examples and/or templates.

All readers of this book will received a quick, accessible, thorough, and proven tool to learn or refresh the business concepts needed to write a successful, relevant, and fundable business plan. Anyone interested in building a business plan is encouraged to read every section of this book to benefit from, on a strategic level, the essence of a business degree. Business students who use this as a textbook will be utilizing excellent and state-of-the-art strategies and will transform into productive entrepreneurs as they create their business plan. For business students this book will add a strategic level perspective to all lessons throughout their program. All readers will be able to confidently present a respectable, reasonable, and researched business plan to CEOs and funding sources after they have read and applied the directions provided in this book.

Facing the Unique Challenges of Writing a Business Plan

One of the most challenging issues surrounding building a business plan is that research is often not completed in the order that it is used in the twelve stages of the business plan. This means that building a business plan is not a straight line or linear process. Writers of business plans often have to do research early that will not be used until later in the document, for example as late as Section 6 or 7; then again, later research may be needed for an earlier segment like Section 3.

Additionally, it may be that one section will be written early and then with later research it will be discovered that some of the assumptions from the earlier research are invalidated by later findings. Then the writer needs to go back and update earlier parts with the new information. Remember, the business plan is a "working document" and each section is not finished until the final business plan is put together and complete. This means that the business plan writer will continuously be revising earlier sections as more data is learned and as new ideas "pop-up". Working documents are allowed to be messy, have highlighting, notes, and earmarks (all those can be done in electronic form in Word) as all those are tools that can help to make the end product better.

Please be patient with the process and learn the skill of flexibility and be able to flow back and forth from one section to the next and to rewrite and reevaluate them as needed. This is how most jobs work, especially as moving further up the hierarchal ladder.

This book is designed to walk the reader through the whole process and strategy level research, analysis, and writing for building a business plan. The suggestion is that the writer of the business plan:

1. Prints out and also keeps a copy of the template provided in Chapter 2 of the book on the 12 stages of a business plan on their own computer.
2. Understands that all business plans are unique, but each business plan will have information in each of the 12 sections. Some of the sections will be more critical with more details for some innovations than others. In other words, some sections will only be ten pages long while others may be 50.
3. Reads the entire text book cover to cover and takes within their own copy of the business plan (see #1 above) special and specific comments of the areas that will be critical for the specific innovation.
4. Starts writing the outline for the business plan using the template and filling in what they learn from research.
5. Understands that in order for a business plan to be complete there will need to be a minimum of fifty (most have almost twice that) cited business research sources. Funded business plans are based upon data-driven decision making, not opinions, and data-driven decisions come from research that is current, valid, and cited.

Note to students: Receiving a good grade on earlier papers does not mean that those successful papers can just be cut and pasted into the final business plan document and that the final grade will be passing. Not only are the continuity and connections between sections a critical part of passing the capstone, but the papers/sections should also be updated with continuous research outcome. Under that aspect papers/sections cannot remain the same from when they were first turned in to them being part of the final business plan.

Table of Contents

Prefix

Dr. Helen Eckmann enjoyed a successful business career at Raytheon, Union Bank, and Jazzercise. Starting her own consulting business, James L Consulting, in the early 1990ies she received San Diego Business Woman of the Year from National Association of Women Business Owners (NAWBO) in the capacity in 2009. Helen started her college career later in life and became full-time faculty upon receiving her doctorate degree in 2002. She has always specialized her teaching around the successful business experiences in strategy, innovation, and supply chain.

Helen has received "Teacher of the Year" awards nine times at all three universities where she has taught. She specializes in designing and delivering classes that are practical, serious, and strongly student learning centered. She has a passion for student success. Helen has over 2,500 contacts on LinkedIn, most of those contacts are former students who like to keep her in the loop of their ongoing successes.

As a full-time Faculty and Associate Professor at Brandman University for the past nine years, she had the opportunity to be on the team that developed both, the BBA (Bachelor in Business Administration) and the MBA (Masters in Business Administration) for Brandman University, prior to which she had been full-time faculty at University of San Diego and National University. As the current Vice Chair of the Institute for Supply Management's (ISM) World Wide Ethics Council, she is in direct contact with the business leaders of today. ISM has over 50,000 members from eighty countries. Click this link for more details on ISM: www.ism.ws.

Helen has a strong philanthropic spirit and has been feeding the homeless for two decades. She has volunteered thousands of hours to her professional connections through the Institute of Supply Management, Sanford Burnham Cancer Research Center, and the City of Del Mar. Helen has been married to her husband Jim for thirty years and has four successful children, two sons and two daughters, both of her daughters have received a PhD.

Kerstin Young, BBA and MBA from Brandman University, is one of the most intellectual, collaborative, and hardest working students that Helen had the privilege to teach. Kerstin has a strong research and analytical mind. She has an excellent practical understanding of how businesses work. Her focus is on the broadest scope of business; strategic thinking through the details of developing action plan steps gives her an unusual and thoughtful understanding of business. Thus, Kerstin has the ability and background to view both, the highest levels of business and the details that make things actually work. Kerstin comes from a family dedicated to knowledge and her resultant interest in science and education gives her an interdisciplinary approach to her work. As a native of Kaiserslautern, Germany, Kerstin has a broad global perspective and speaks three languages (English, German and French). She is a passionate animal rights advocate/activist, married to an active duty Air Force member, and currently lives in Southern California.

In 2014 Kerstin was in Helen's BBA (Bachelors of Business Administration) Capstone class at Brandman University and distinguished herself as an incredible thinker, researcher, analyst, and writer. She also gave salient and timely help to other students in the class. This is not common, unfortunately, as many highly driven and intelligent students do not have the patience, time, or desire to help others. After taking the BBA Capstone Kerstin suggested to Helen that a textbook for the class was to be developed. She had a great idea and like it often happens when someone has a great idea, they are asked to help to make it happen; so Helen kept this in mind and eventually did.

As luck would have it, in 2016 Kerstin was scheduled in Helen's MBA (Masters of Business Administration) Capstone class at Brandman University and once again distinguished herself as a scholar, team player, and human being. She was another time ready, willing, and able to help her fellow students. At the end of the class in heartfelt communications about Kerstin's success, the idea of co-publishing came to life as if it was "meant to be". Kerstin and Helen first developed the BBA capstone textbook and Kerstin has helped every step of the way. She brought a practical student-centered approach from beginning to end for each section of this book. Helen stated, "I have been blessed by her and I know that all who read and use this book will be equally blessed. I have to admit that Kerstin has a better understanding of APA than I do; she gets down into the fine print."

Dr. Helen Eckmann and Kerstin Young have proven to be a dynamic and successful team in the development of business books on strategy and business plan development. They co-created this book and one previously, to assist students to understand how to recognize an opportunity and how to create value from that opportunity - in short, create a business plan!

Introduction

Writing a business plan is an adventure and over ninety percent of individuals who begin this journey are amazed eventually how smart and capable they are! However, some people who have great ideas for businesses often lack the know-how of how to turn their good ideas into a workable plan of action. This book will provide the steps necessary to produce a real, practical, and actionable business plan. Once all of the processes are completed in this book the entrepreneur will be able to distinguish if their "good idea" makes economic sense. Thousands of dollars can be saved and hours of "wishing" can be turned into clear knowledge and understanding if a "good idea" can and will actually work.

There will be certain concepts and aspects that are going to be repeated and mentioned continually throughout this book to assist the understanding and writing of a business plan. These critical reminders might be stressed in a few sections so that a clear understanding and the knowledge of the gravity of identifying factors like demographics, financial opportunities, the product and/or service, and the need for the innovation is formed.

In this book repetition of critical issues and frequent examples are used for the benefit of the reader. However, it is imperative that the business plan does not display repetition or examples. A business plan should only have key points, references, supporting pictures, graphs, and references to prove the value of the business, and not extraneous examples. Furthermore, it is the duty of the writer to be clear and concise. There should be no surprise questions about the business plan by the reader of the business plan as all areas of opportunity, industry, and risk have been completely and clearly highlighted in the business plan.

Readers of this book will notice that there are very few appendices to it, which should be the same in the business plan. The idea is to put all of the information needed right at a reader's fingertips; accordingly, funding sources or CEOs will not flip back and forth in a business plan as they will want all relevant data easily viewed. Additions like appendices should be surplus information but not essential for understanding the business plan or document.

One of the greatest resource that entrepreneurs may want to engage in for business plan and financial plan development success is the FREE Website from SCORE at www.Score.org. The Mission Statement for Score is: "We connect entrepreneurs with mentors to help you build your business with free business advice." Score also provides all of the templates authors will need for the financial section (more on financial reporting requirements in below). For a preview on the variety of financial templates this is the link: https://www.score.org/resource/business-planning-financial-statements-template-gallery. Once all the research and analysis for all the papers or sections in this class are completed, business plan writers will find that all of the needed tools for the completion of the business plan are indeed available at the Score website. If this book is being used as a textbook, student entrepreneurs will need to check with their faculty to find out if Score is an appropriate resource for their university.

The following link is to a business plan template that the Score website offers: https://www.score.org/resource/business-plan-template-startup-business. This is a good place to start. Nevertheless, student entrepreneurs must also meet all their school course requirements, usually found on the Learning Management Systems (like Blackboard) but commonly in the Syllabus. So if Score templates differ from or conflict with the course material, students must always follow the course materials first.

Even though that academic students are required by the instructor to fulfil their business plan in papers that will come together as the final plan, it is highly recommended for entrepreneurs to do the same as well. To divide an 80 to 150-page business plan into sectional papers makes the project much more manageable and less overwhelming. It is therefore advisable that entrepreneurs follow all timelines for section/paper-writing as well as all other suggestions that are designed towards students.

It is also interesting and important to note that this book can generally be read like a novel, front to back, which is atypical for a text book. However, business plan writers will find that reading this book will work more like a manual where the book is read from front to back and then frequently referenced throughout the writing of the plan. As each individual section of the business plan is written (marketing, operations, etc.) it will be helpful to review the corresponding section in the book and apply the details and follow the hints and helps provided. It is important to read this book early and often during the business plan development as the encouragement and the keys for success and answers to most questions are provided inside.

CHAPTER I – The 12 Sections of the Business Plan

Remember every business plan will be unique and will depend upon the specific innovation; and yet there are certain standards that must be met. A business plan should have at least twelve sections; some might have more, depending on the innovation and business (but everything that is listed below will need to be covered with research and analysis). Knowing these sections is "prep-work" for building a business plan. As research and analysis develop for the innovation, knowing what information is required for the business plan will speed up the research or outright enable it.

It is suggested that the following twelve steps be copied and pasted and put into a separate Word document on the personal computer of the business plan writer. This list is an excellent start for the outline for the business plan. Some find that in addition to printing out the twelve steps and having them handy as writing continues, they also assist in narrowing down the research elements.

Each of these twelve steps will need to have citations from the research that applies to the individual innovation. Following this template will bring a comfort early on in the process of business plan writing as the formatting provided is excellent for starting the outline, as well as providing structure for the research.

The business plan needs to be written in a Word document and should not contain animations or other technology or applications that have the potential to confuse the reader or worse to not work as planned. It is important that the reader of the business plan can easily access the business plan from a variety of computers and that it can pass through safety and security features like firewalls and antivirus programs. Furthermore, do not assume that funding sources are "technology savvy". Be sure that the business plan is written to satisfy the needs and wants of the intended reader (funding source, professor, friends and family members, etc.).

Every one of the twelve sections has been placed on its own page so that the business plan writer will be reminded that each section in the business plan starts on a new page as well. This also provides room for additional research ideas and to take notes. When done with research and writing some of these twelve sections will be twenty to thirty pages long while others can be shorter. Traditionally Sections 3 through 10 and section 12 are each twenty to forty pages long because they include research and analyses, resulting in graphics, charts, and financials. The Executive Summary, the Mission and Vision, and the Conclusions are often one to two pages, however.

Most commonly the struggles for business plan writers do not lie within these sections themselves, but within the understanding of the underlying concepts and analysis required to build a successful business plan. The remainder of this book will help business plans writers to see the twelve steps or sections, and yet more importantly focus and understand on how to successfully apply the fundamentals of current business practices to their business venture.

This is an excellent for business plan templates and examples: http://www.inc.com/larry-kim/top-10-business-plan-templates-you-can-download-free.html.

The traditional twelve sections are the following:

1. Executive Summary

The executive summary will be part of the outline, but will not be written until all the research has been completed and all of the other sections have been finished. With that, the executive summary, although positioned first in the project, should actually be written last. That way the business plan writer knows what to summarize. Writing it earlier will cause it to tend towards a traditional introduction and will not cover the whole scope of the research and analysis.

However, it is good to know that the purpose of an executive summary is to write a brief description of the plan that allows the reader to gain the essence of the entire plan in less than two pages. Consider who the intended reader and judge will be of the success of the business plan. If this is written for an academic grade, then meet all of the criteria that the instructor has outlined; if the audience is a funding source, then meet all of their criteria. The executive summary (and in fact the whole business plan) needs to target and be appealing to the intended reader.

If the business plan is intended to give a busy executive the key information and lead the reader to the sections that will answer the executive's primary questions. It is not an introduction to the plan, as it may have been written in typical papers. The executive summary is meant to raise the interest of the executive reading it to continue reading and evaluating the business plan. Keep in mind, this might be the only section the executive would read; if not interesting, they might dismiss the rest. The executive summary is always at least one full page but never more than two pages long. Once again, write this last!

The elements of an Executive Summary are:

- Usually starts with "There is a need" and is backed up by data. This includes a description of the unsatisfied need that creates the business opportunity and innovation desire
- Purpose of the plan (attract investors, bring a new innovation to a specific, identified, and cited market, etc.)
- Introduction to market opportunity – what is the innovation, what is the industry, what is the value that it brings
- Some highlights of the demographics of the customer
- Briefly show why the innovation is a financially sound business idea

2. Mission & Vision Statement & Innovation Description

The mission and vision should be carefully crafted. There should be sufficient evidence of how operational, financial, management, and marketing plans are executed in light of the innovation's mission and vision. This should be about two pages long and remember the mission statement should be short enough to fit on a t-shirt. The vision statement is sometimes a paragraph with bullets. The innovation description should take up another page to a page and a half and should be focusing on the unique opportunity that the innovation brings to the marketplace. This language should be clean, clear, and easy to understand for people outside of the industry (as funding sources are often not "insiders").

Company Description (proposed new organization):

- Type of Business and Legal Structure (e.g., LLC, sole proprietorship)
- Clear, concise and interesting description of what the innovation is uniquely bringing to the marketplace
- Distinctive Core Competencies, overview of the location, financial viability, etc.
- Consumer demographic that is interested in buying/using this new product or service
- If there is any technology include simple, clean, and clear language to describe it

3. Industry & Trends Analysis

- (state of the industry, market research, barriers to entry, identifying competitors, identifying market niche, expert advice, competitive analysis, strategic positioning)
- This is the section where writers need to perform a "preliminary SWOT analysis" that will need further data and research. It is also the first long section that is usually ten to twenty pages long with more than ten sources. Often this section includes three to four graphs describing the industry, competition, and industry evolution, all with cited data from academic and business sources:
  - The history of the industry
  - Size of the industry
  - Industry evolution
  - The trend--where the industry is expected to be in five to ten years
  - The key players in the industry (those who do something like this well and those who do not, something different)
  - Perform a competitive advantage analysis (what is currently available so in the next section it can be shown how the competition)
  - Barriers and challenges to entering the market
  - Environmental scan
  - Significant factors in the macro environment

  The section presents a clear statement of the opportunities and threats through preliminary SWOT analysis. The SWOT analysis connects to the research and results in data-driven decision making. Other issues include but are not limited to:

  - Copyrights, patents, & intellectual property rights
  - Research & development activities
  - Failures in the industry
  - Opportunities
  - Changes in the market
  - Description if the innovation is a product or a service or a products & a service, what this product means for the industry
  - Research & development activities

4. Strategic Positioning, Strategic Intent (Measurable Goals) with Competition Strengths & Weaknesses (using Main SWOT Analysis & other matrices)

- This section is also ten to twenty pages long and often includes graphs for the Main SWOT analysis and other measurable goals. This means that the SWOT analysis that was performed in the previous section will now become more thorough and more complete. This section includes:
    - Exactly where the innovation will fit into the current marketplace
    - Explain how strategy will be developed for success
    - Evidence of strategic & critical thinking
    - A strategic plan
    - Details of how the Strategic Intent will influence the business & will be assimilated into the workplace
    - Graphs of the competition with the history of successes & failures that connect directly or indirectly to the proposed innovation
    - Flexibility & agility for strategic changes that will be necessary as the marketplace grows, diminishes, or changes

5. Product / Service

- (define product or service, what makes the product worthwhile, liability concerns, expert advice)
- This section is often around ten to twenty pages long and explains what and how the product or service will actually do. This is almost always accompanied by graphics to make the product and/or service clear to the funding source or reader of the business plan. Most good business plans have about five to six graphics in this section. If this section is not crystal clear, then the funding source or the reader will lose interest and not continue reading. The section should cover:
    - What the product or service does for the consumer
    - Description & graphics of how this product or service will impact the consumer
    - Description of the product variances that are provided initially or in the future (e.g. can it come in pink later, or can it be made smaller in the next iteration, etc.)
    - It is not recommended to put animations in this section as they often do not work & cause the reader to lose interest
    - What it looks like, smells like, feels like, sounds like, tastes like (all that apply)?
    - How does the position in the <u>Product</u> Life Cycle affect this Business Plan?
    - How does the position in the <u>Industry</u> Life Cycle affect this Business Plan?
    - Describe the "Cradle to Cradle" impacts for design production through recycle
    - Begin to describe how the product or service will be branded (refer to more details in the marketing section)

6. Management Plan

- (hiring projections, board of directors or advisors, outside professionals, licenses, expert advice)

  This section is sometimes confused as a "leadership" section which is not the purpose of the management plan. The management plan is directly related to the mission and vision of the company and is why, who, when, and how all tasks that are performed in the routine actions of the business.

  Management & ownership:

  - Board of Directors & rationale for members
  - Management staff structure - Organizational chart
  - Key managers
  - Plans to attract, develop, & retain key personnel
  - Future additions to the current management team
  - Compensation & reward plans (based upon Indeed.com data)
  - Training & motivation plan (financial & otherwise)
  - Insurance plans & costs
  - Government rules & regulations that might apply
  - An overall management plan that outlines how work will flow, be distributed, assigned, and assessed
  - This section often applies the "SMART Goals" information found later in this book
  - Answer Drucker's Five Questions as they relate to the innovation & business: http://www.inc.com/peter-economy/5-essential-questions-entrepreneurs.html

7. Marketing Plan

- Connects to all ways that the customer is defined, researched, developed, and maintained (this includes defining the product, defining the customers, selling prices, market placing/segmentation, promotion, follow-up plan, & expert advice)
- This section, like all parts of the business plan, is based upon data-driven decision making and has citations. It is often thirty to fifty pages long and has four to five graphs (often created using SmartArt, most often for Competition, five Ps, Demand, Communication Plan, Sales Strategy). Remember the Marketing, Management, and Operations plans all must demonstrate collaboration and correlation with each other.
- Use http://www.fedstats.gov/ for more information.
- This section addresses in the least the following:

  - What is the competitive advantage that this business will create?
  - Major characteristics of the target market (what does the customer look like?)
  - How will this innovation be branded?
  - Marketing Plan Analysis
  - What is the demand of this target market?
  - Nature of the competition
  - What are total sales to this market in geographic area?
  - What are total sales expected in five years, in ten years?
  - What percentage of this demand does this business expect to capture?
  - Provides evidence that all of the five Ps have been addressed
  - What is the FMOT (first moment of truth) and SMOT (second moment of truth) for the customer
  - Communication plan, both internally and externally
  - Overall marketing strategy
    - Specific marketing mix
    - Strengths & weaknesses in ability to satisfy target market needs
  - Channels of distribution (that connect directly to the Operations Plan)
  - Sales strategy (Customer Relationship Management Program or Plan)

- Product & service cost & the rationale for that cost & comparison of like product costs
- Competitive dynamics

8. Operations Plan

- (operations for product or service from the beginning to the end of the supply chain (Cradle to Cradle) of the supply chain, technology, expert advice)
- This section is usually about twenty to thirty pages long, with four or five graphs (usually for suppliers, service, and delivery procedures), process flow chart, SRM and transportation. It must dovetail with the Management and Marketing plans. Remember, the operations plan explains and gives the details of the "story of how goods and services flow through the organization". This section usually has ten to thirty cited business sources within the industry of the innovation or other related industries. Examples may be cited from "best in class" operations and supply chain processes found in very different industries, but the applications must be clear. **Remember that there are always supplier considerations with both a product and a service.**

  Key suppliers, customers, & operations plans, at least:

  - List of potential suppliers
  - Production & service delivery procedures
  - Supply Chain process flow chart (how goods & services will flow from the supplier all the way through the organization to the customer). These are some examples: https://www.google.com/search?q=process+flow+chart&tbm=isch&tbo=u&source=univ&sa=X&ved=0ahUKEwiwj_qUwI3QAhXHh1QKHdwABsQQsAQISg&biw=1920&bih=97
  - Overall Supplier Relationship Management (SRM) to include all ethical considerations
  - Supply Chain
  - Logistics
  - Packaging
  - Transportation
  - Physical Plant Layout
  - Organizational chart for supply chain (if more than three people work in operations)

- DMAIC – apply DMAIC in the operations section – demonstrate that this can be applied, not described, to the innovation
- Ethical considerations (respond on questions on page 58)
- Description of how the supply chain will be developed to create: time to market, quality, innovation, or cost (it is impossible to build a supply chain to receive each of the four in equal measure as these are mutually exclusive (for example: time to market is more expensive))

9. Financial Plan

- (income statement, balance sheet, cash flow statement, personal financial statement [not included in student plan – but students need to be aware of this requirement], financial ratios, forecasts, expert advice)
- The financial plan is often the longest section of the business plan and includes Excel spreadsheets that are copied and pasted directly into the Word document in the financial section. These financial spreadsheets are accompanied by written explanations that give a clear analysis of what data is found in the spread sheets and their interpretation, conclusion, and meaning. It is never acceptable to include spreadsheets or data without a clearly written explanation of what the financial data means to the innovation, the investor, and the industry.

It is important that the innovation shows a profit within the first eighteen months. If that is not the case, explanations of why not need to be included. If there is to be no real profit in the first eighteen months, then the innovation may need to be broken down into phases. If the changes are made to offer the innovation in phases then the Management, Marketing, and Operations plans must be adjusted. The Excel sheets that always have to be presented within the financials section are: Startup expenses, 12-month profit and loss, and break-even analysis. Once again, the financial statements are not just found in the appendix section, which is all the way at the end of the business plan, as funding sources do not want to take that much time to go there; the spreadsheets are copied and pasted into the appropriate section of the business plan.

Financial Analysis

- Funds required & their sources
- Current funding requirements
- Funding requirements over the next three years (key ratios to focus on)
- Use of funds
- Loss control
- Explain how the Six Steps of Economic Decision Making apply to the innovation

- Financial statements for first three (3) years (monthly first year and annually for years two and three) (may use template)
- Start-up expenses
- 12-month profit & loss
- Break-even analysis
- Income statements
- Balance sheets
- Cash flow statements
- Determine capital requirements
- Determine funding sources

10. Action Plan

(steps to take to implement business plan, including performance evaluation criteria)

This is detailed and contains information for all action steps from most of the twelve sections of the business plan. For example, if in the marketing plan there is a promotion proposed, then the action steps for designing, manufacturing, and distributing the promotion would be included in the action plan. This section is always more than ten pages long and contains timelines. The Action Plan assesses and explains who (or which position) does what, how, and when. This is often directly connected to the Management, Marketing, and Operations Plans. This section always contains a graphic and clear explanations.

11. Conclusions & Recommendations

This section is usually about two pages long and should directly connect to the "promises made" in the executive summary. For example, if it is mentioned in the executive summary that the new service will be ground breaking for a new demographic, then the conclusion and recommendations should focus in on that promise.

- Conclude why the business is a viable business
- Connects directly to the Mission & Vision
- Rationale for why the business plan should begin at this time
- Clearly restates the financial value & opportunity that the innovation brings to the marketplace

12. Reference & Appendices Sections

References

The reference section will include at least 50 sources (many have more than 100) for research of the business plan an APA citation will be provided for each source). Remember that the eight sections of the business plan that are data-driven all have sources from extensive research. With that, ten from each of those sections would already combine to 80 sources.

This section continues with the Arabic numbering of pages. Only sources of information that have actually been cited in the project are included here. (see APA sample paper https://owl.english.purdue.edu/owl/resource/560/18/)

Appendices

The appendices continue with the Arabic numbering of pages from the previous section. (see APA sample paper: https://owl.english.purdue.edu/owl/resource/560/18/)

Examples for appendices include but are not limited to:

- Key employee resumes, product & advertising samples, press clippings
- First impression collateral (e.g. cover letters for sources of income, brand, printing, design, charts, graphs & tables, multimedia presentations, etc.)
- Information that creates capital (market research, communication plan, financing, websites, trade groups and associations, etc.)

The above twelve sections are required for the business plan and therefore its development. Reading forward in the text book it will become apparent that business plan development is not a linear process and requires critical thinking skills (which will be defined later on). As each section of the business plan is developed and additional information is gathered and understood, frequent reassessments of the previous sections that have already been developed will need to take place. Thus, business plan writing is essentially thinking and re-thinking, researching and re-researching, and writing and rewriting.

The information in the chapters below is offered in the way that the processes of business plans need to be considered and completed; the information above demonstrates the way that the business plan will be presented.

CHAPTER II - Business Plan Applications & Innovative Ways of Thinking

Developing Good Ideas for Innovations

This part of the business plan development, or better said its prep work, is really about creativity; it is about seeing a need and demonstrating that need in form of a product or service. This section is not always intuitive and many business plan writers ignore the first steps concerning innovative ways of thinking.

Below three different ways are presented to spark creativity and to come up with or refine a good business plan idea. These tools to kick start a creative mind are: Mind Maps, Morning Pages, and Time-Outs. There are many ways to encourage one's mind into coming up with good ideas and those given are just three of them. Watch this Ted Talk from Sting https://www.ted.com/talks/sting_how_i_started_writing_songs_again?language=en to learn more about that. Also view this YouTube video by Dr. Jan Jackson and Professor Emeritus at Brandman University: https://www.youtube.com/watch?v=nbFO3I6QlmI.

To begin a **mind map** just take a piece of paper and some crayons, a pen, or a pencil (assorted colors do help) and write "Business Plan" in the middle in a circle and then write all pertinent major categories in "bubbles" around the words "Business Plan" (students might want to look at the 12 parts of the business plan) for the bubbles. Stop and look for a minute and consider if there are any missing major categories, any that make sense and should be added. The mind map should look something like this:

Keep in mind that mind maps can also be created on the computer and do not necessarily have to be shaped with pen and paper. Whatever tool is preferred by the creator is suitable for this project. This mind map was found by simply googling the term "mind map" but many more are out there: https://www.google.com/search?site=&tbm=isch&source=hp&biw=1920&bih=971&q=business+strategy+mind+map+by+hand&oq=business+strategy+mind+map+by+hand&gs_l=img.12...50839.53649.3.55553.18.18.0.

0.0.0.117.1160.17j1.18.0....0...1ac.1.64.img..1.0.0.VVSxvgC5OKU#imgrc=402Z2ZglvtFdYM%3A.

For a mind map for the innovation, it is advised to start a new mind map for every idea and its development. Do not try to merge the ideas, just use another piece of paper and begin again as new and different ideas pop up. Idea seekers may want to carry the mind map around with them during the day as inspiration can come from anywhere, at any time, and often times does. Once the major categories have been established, add some words below the bubbles that could become some of the major subheadings in the business plan.

On a side note, when anyone starts a new project, a new job, or any new endeavor, writing out a mind map is a great idea to help to focus on the strategic view of what they are trying to accomplish. Many people get lost in the details (the dancefloor view, more on that on page 95) and forget the larger picture (the balcony view, more on that on page 95). A mind map helps people to focus on the balcony or strategic level.

Morning pages are meant to allow creativity to be captured when it is fresh, in the morning, immediately after waking up. Anybody who uses this tool should have pen and paper by the bed side and start writing as soon as they wake. Thoughts can be captured without any outline or restriction, whatever comes to mind should be notated. Then later on, the author should sift through and see if there is anything that can be used in the business plan to any extent. A great summary about morning pages can be found in the appendix on page 175.

Time-outs are recovery time from every-day life and are supposed to allow for creativity to form and flow. Time-outs are essentially "me-time" and can therefore be anything that gets people's mind out of stress and other distractors to the free flow of creativity. It can be really anything, from walks in nature, over massages, manicures, and pedicures, to a hobby. More information on time-outs can be found in the document in the appendix on page 173.

To finish up this section on idea development it needs to be mentioned that there is a difference between the vision and the mission statement. The vision statement should be short (able to fit on a t-shirt) and stands for (describes) the reason for the innovation; it is the future of the innovation, the end state. The mission statement is usually longer and entails the explanation of how to reach the final goals for the business (plan). The mission can change with internal and external circumstances, but the vision does not. In short, the how (the path to achieve the ultimate company goal - vision) can and is expected to be adjusted and changed, but the what (the ultimate goal – vision) is not. Here is a link to get more detail on the difference of vision and mission: https://www.psychologytoday.com/blog/smartwork/201004/vision-and-mission-whats-the-difference-and-why-does-it-matter.

Considering the "Two Feet of Innovation"

Innovation is a practical creative idea that is ready to be implemented. Innovation is different than creativity in as far as that creativity is an idea, but an innovation is a good idea that is ready for implementation or execution. Innovation can be many different things, however, for simplicity use the "Two Feet of Innovation" by Dr. Eckmann to make some distinctions. It will be important to understand and use "Two Feet" as a tool to formulate the innovation. Additional information and application will be discussed on page 116. This tool is broken down like this:

Brand new idea; something that has not been done before. For example, the first cell phone was such an innovation.

It is a major jump or process improvement for an existing product or service. An example is when the first laptop was produced. It was still a computer but it had been innovated to a whole new level. Now, the newest iteration of a cell phone is not an innovation (slightly faster, slightly lighter). The smartphone, conversely, with its new functions and features would have been an innovation at inception. Furthermore, applying a concept from one industry to another can be a "left foot innovation". For example, using a 3-D Printer is not an innovation, however using a 3-D Printer to make "test" hearts for doctors to practice on before open heart surgery is a "left foot" innovation, as it is taking an existing technology and applying it in a wholly new way. This "3-D Printer" innovation was a part of the dramatic (and highly innovative) television Show "Pure Genius" (http://www.imdb.com/title/tt5500906/).

Also, for the purpose of an innovative business plan it is not an innovation to open up a new branch of an existing service. For example, to open up a Gap store in a city that previously has not had a Gap store is not an innovation (neither right nor left foot) and is therefore not sufficient for an innovation as it is an expansion. With a clear literature review (more on this on page 66) it is easier to see if the innovation idea is "right or left foot" or if it is just an expansion of something that already exists. Determine early through research the authenticity of the innovation so that as little time as possible is wasted.

Comparing Differences of Products & Services

The vast majority of business plans needs to be extremely clear if the purpose of the business plan is to create an innovation that is either a product or service or both. It is important to understand the distinction between a product and a service and to make that clear in the business plan, whether it is a product, a service, or both. Sometimes during the process of developing a business plan that was initially intended to just present a product idea it becomes apparent that a part of business plan will need to cover services as well as they would naturally accompany the product. This means that the entire business plan would be rethought from the beginning, making the mission and vision, all marketing, management, and operations plans to include both, the service and the product. The reverse could also be true as initially both a product and service were intended to be offered and with more research it could be determined that it would be better (cheaper and more efficient) to outsource the service section to an existing company.

Once again, the business plan will need to start, develop, and end with an action plan for a product, a service, or both and nothing contradictory can be included. All sections of the business plan remain a "working document" until the entire business plan has to be turned in to the instructor or to the funding sources. Business plan developers need to realize that earlier sections of the business plan will often need to be reworked as more research and data are collected and analyzed. Students who have completed and received an "A" on, for example, their marketing plan, still may need to go back and change that section as they gain more insight into the subject. It is recommended to keep all documents that have been approved and start new versions as changes are made, because sometimes the original version ends up being stronger than subsequent versions. That process will keep all options open. However, it is crucial that all versions are kept organized and easily accessible.

The following are the distinctions between product and service:

Goods are: basically objects or products which have to be manufactured, stored, transported, marketed, and sold (Bhasin, 2016). For example: televisions, shoes, lamps, etc.

Services are: output of individuals and they can be a collective or individualistic action or performance by an individual (Bhasin, 2016). For example: financial services, legal maintenance, pet care, etc.

An example for the product-service combination is ATMs. They are hardware or products, but changing a code for ATMs to be more efficient is a service. If a business plan is offering both, ATMs and software updates, there is a contribution to both, a product and a service and the research and analysis within the business plan have to display both as well. However, it needs to be considered, offering both, a product and a service, is a lot more complicated and the business plan will require additional research and analysis. Nevertheless, it might be necessary to offer a service with the product in order to sell the product at all. An example for that would be, if the innovation is a new water treatment system, there might be a need to offer servicing that product in order for people to feel comfortable purchasing it. This is usually true for large and complicated or technical innovations. Envision an every-day product like a car without any opportunity to have it serviced or repaired; or an insulin pump without any doctors knowing how to set and replace it.

Defining Products & Services

Much of this material will be used to help write Section 5 of the business plan, "Products and Services". It is important that the definition of the business includes a detailed description of what is being offered. Be very clear if the business offers a product, a service, or both. Next, be very clear to describe the specifics of what is unique and what brings value. If the reader of the business plan has to interpret what he or she is reading about the product or service, then two things can happen and they are both negative: over-interpretation or under-interpretation of the innovation:

1. The reader who over-interprets might invest in a business that was not intended and further down the road there will be a major disagreement resulting in financial loss for the sources of funding and a resulting loss

of reputation for both the funding source as well as the writer of the business plan.

2. The reader who under-interprets might not invest at all because they might not understand the proposed business.

The explanation of the product or service is usually accompanied by a graphic or other visual aid and uses words that an insider to the industry would know and appreciate, but also uses words that someone outside of the industry can makes sense of. Most authors write and rewrite the product and service section many times before the final draft is complete. The product and service section will have information that has been gathered from all of the research (thus as more information gained, this section will be upgraded). For example, when the operations section is complete and more information is learned about how to manufacture a product then some of those key distinctive points would be added to the description of the product or service. Another example, as information is gained on the demographics, that information might be critical to add to the product and service section.

Developing an Innovation Description

This part will also aide in the writing of Section 5 of the business plan, "Product and Service". Developing an innovation description is an iterative process (much like the SWOT analysis above). This means as more research is completed in the field in which the innovation lives, the innovative description will be improved and refined. More information on the industry, trends, the innovation, and the financial data will create a clearer understanding of the innovation and this information will be used to update the innovation description. The information needs to be clear to an outsider (many marketing campaigns are targeted to a 9th grade learning level), so do not use big words or words that are industry specific. Industry specific terms need to be used correctly. For example, there is a significant difference between electronic and electric. So use the right terms, it is more than just semantics (remember to use jargon sparingly and if used, explain and define). The innovation description will be written early and needs to be evaluated again over the time of the course of writing.

Begin developing an innovation description by reviewing other innovations in the industry or the history of products and services that compare, then look at some of the competitors or companies in the industry and see if there are interesting and helpful innovation descriptions. Look further at the mission and vision and start to find the keywords that would be used in the innovation description. Suggestions are to use as many action words as possible like “developing”, “creating”, “analyzing”, “offering”, and (of course) “innovating”. Also be sure to make it clear if the innovation is a product, a service, or both. So if building a product and the product was an infrared thermometer to measure temperatures in the kitchens for home cooking, then the innovation description would include words like:

- Product
- Small kitchen appliances
- Home safety innovation
- Affordable
- Cutting edge
- Innovations in kitchen essentials
- Small electronics
- Infrared thermometer
- Easy to use
- Improve cooking skills
- Save money on food (less waste)
- Children’s safety

So once the list is complete (aim for at least twenty words) then take those words and work up a few possible ways to combine the words to describe the innovation. This can be fun and it is part of the business plan that could take family, friends, or coworkers opinions into consideration as they can vote on which sets of words are most appealing. Be sure to keep the ultimate consumer in mind (this is a perspective that should always be kept in the forefront; after all, the product or service needs to bring value and that only happens if the product or service can be sold). Often the innovation description is used in a diversity of marketing materials.

Branding the Innovation

Much of this information will be used in the Section 7 of the business plan, for “Marketing”; this information will also be useful to craft the executive summary. Any business plan is designed to “sell” an idea, the innovation, based upon data-driven decision making, to the CEO (usually) of a company or a financial executive (at a bank, for example). This means it is important that the business plan has a professional and marketing look and feel to it. That level of professionalism is accomplished in a variety of ways: by using business terms correctly, having a consistent but not repeated theme (there is a difference between repeated and repetitive, whereas repeated is a positive and repetitive a negative attribute), and/or topic appropriate color pallet throughout the entire business plan. All those parts will be discussed in detail and a roadmap to success will be provided throughout this book.

Even though the instructor and hypothetically the CEO of a Fortune 500 company, an investor, the head lending officer at a financial institution, or any other executive and decision maker are the audience for the business plan, it is important to describe the innovation in terms that the general public could understand. For example, if the student or entrepreneur is developing a specific technology he or she has to be sure that the words used are comprehensible and will explain the concept in detail (pictures might be added). The executive will not approve and fund what he or she does not understand. Remember, most CEOs or executive decision makers are not strong on the details and entrepreneurs cannot assume that the innovation lies within their field of expertise.

A great article to learn more about branding, can be found here: https://www.entrepreneur.com/article/77408.

Writing a Business Plan as a Capstone Project

There are many reasons for innovators, entrepreneurs, and students to write a business plan. Many, if not most, business schools use the business plan format as a vehicle for students to become entrepreneurs and as such to demonstrate their ability to apply the academic material learned by the end of a business program.

Students who are getting a business degree have to think like an entrepreneur. Students gain such excellent skills in a business degree they often become entrepreneurs and implement their capstone business plans into working and successful endeavors. For both, the student and the entrepreneur, the business plan is the gateway to taking "Ideas to Action". Business plans have a wide scope as they demonstrate how a business operates in both, domestic and international, contexts.

Topics of analysis include: how an industry operates in a variety of environments, how to analyze internal firm resources, product placing, competencies and competitive advantages, and weaknesses. Additionally, business plan authors will analyze and apply the issues of outsourcing, mergers, acquisitions and joint ventures, and the integration of functional and behavioral knowledge in the formulation and implementation of firm strategies and tactics. Those with business degrees and well researched, analyzed, and written business plans are often able to offer their service as a consultant.

Exploring Adaptive & Technical Challenges

The following section will continue to assist the business plan writer with innovative thinking and to assess the proposed innovation. This concept provides a way of looking at the strategic level of a particular innovation and also to view the "grass roots" implementation, adaptive and technical challenges. Please be patient as you read this next section because thinking this way is not always intuitive, but once grasped it can create stronger strategic thinking skills.

An adaptive challenge refers to a problem for which there is no set pattern for solution. Heifetz and Laurie (1997) describe it as systemic problems without ready answers. It is conundrum that has not been solved yet and will take the cooperation of many individuals to solve, often over long periods of time. By contrast, a technical challenge is one where set patterns, protocols, or procedures already exist or can be used with slight modifications in order to solve the challenge effectively. For the consideration of the business plan, is it critical to examine what are the issues that are adaptive and what are the issues that are technical. Read further to consider more about the differences between adaptive and technical challenges.

Example of adaptive technical: A favorite example of both types is embodied in virtually every episode of the HBO television series "Game of Thrones", which features seven families in a fantasy medieval time setting that are all struggling for power and control. The characters are involved in struggles between and within families, within themselves and others, personal and interpersonal. As troubling as the resulting wars that arise are, they present, at base, technical challenges. Protocols and strategies for war are pretty well established and procedures are put in motion with rapid-fire instructions. At the same time, the personal lives of the main characters are usually in turmoil. A romantic conflict cannot be solved in one episode and will require repeated efforts over several weeks. Problems seem to arise between fathers and sons that result in patricide. A financial crisis or a family situation will likewise require appreciable time to solve, involving lengthy discussions and efforts. These personal relationships are the adaptive challenges in this program, while war seems to be more technical. This is counter-intuitive and is an example of why the examination and classification of adaptive and technical challenges are so important.

More examples of adaptive technical: This example comes from the military's efforts to incorporate female members into virtually all aspects of military service, including combat. In the past women were restricted from many combat position and the unintended consequences of "shielding women from combat" was that many women did not qualify for promotions in the military. This created a very low percentage of women in the higher ranks. Now, the "devil is in the details" as women are to be incorporated into all jobs. Women, and some men, have long chafed under the combat restrictions, which allowed women to serve in combat zones, often under fire, but prevented them from officially holding combat positions, including in the infantry, which remain crucial to career advancement. Women have often said that by not recognizing their real service, the military has unfairly held them back. The entire article can be found here: http://www.nytimes.com/2015/12/04/us/politics/combat-military-women-ash-carter.html?_r=0. Women will be required to meet all standards to be able to serve in combat zones. This is going to be an adaptive challenge as this has never been done before. There will be mistakes made and the road will be difficult, as this adaptive challenge requires that the military, the women and men both, with rank and without, to be patient but focused.

Yet another example is the War on Drugs: Drug use and abuse are an enormous challenge and drain upon society and its resources; from law enforcement, over crime and family impacts, to economic loss, to name only a few. How will we solve this enormous issue? Stiffer criminal penalties? Education about the dangers of drug use? Family training? School interventions? Lift restrictions on the penalties for personal marijuana use? The appointment of a sole American "Drug Czar" to fight this epidemic and expect him or her to create all of the change necessary is an unrealistic goal and impractical strategy. It would be an idealistic approach for the power of that lone appointee to solve this adaptive challenge as the drug problem in America will only be solved by many minds working in concert over many years.

A last example is the War on Terrorism. An effective solution is airline security after 9/11 as it presents elements of strategies needed for both, adaptive and technical challenges. Many of us have seen evidence of "beefed up" security measures, deployment of air marshals aboard commercial jetliners, and federal security screeners rather than private contractors. Proposals also exist to revamp airline procedures to isolate the flight deck from the rest of the aircraft, including bulletproof doors, installation of pass-through slots for food for the flight crew, and fitting of separate toilet facilities for the flight crew, or at least some form of protected cockpit door procedures. These steps present aspects of both technical and adaptive challenges: Deploying the National Guard to the airports is immediate and has features of a technical solution; strategically changing aircraft designs, retrofitting flight decks, and even changing the way flight crews work with cabin attendants may be more systemic, hence an adaptive challenge. Heifetz and Linsky (2002) point out the adaptive challenges demand several leadership techniques be utilized to address them, including involving all the stakeholders, from the board room, to the loading dock personnel. In short, all stakeholders should be involved to figure out what is the "long standing behavior pattern" (p. 124).

A Cautionary to Consider for Adaptive Technical Challenges

Continuing with the strategic and innovative ways of thinking from adaptive and technical, the following cautionary tale is offered. In the midst of a crisis there is often a rush and urgency to find solutions. This will most likely happen with the writing or implementation of any business plan. More often than not the quick fixes are technical, driven by the tyranny of the urgency. The Heifetz article points out the importance of addressing adaptive challenges with adaptive solutions. There a hundreds of hasty solutions that not only did not solve the problems, but also had the effect of making the difficulties worse (for example building a wall between Mexico and the United States). With that understanding, business plans need to make sure a technical problem is matched with a technical solution and an adaptive challenge is correctly diagnosed as such and met with adaptive strategies and, ultimately, resolutions.

Now consider the two levels of strategic analysis for both, dancefloor and balcony view, for the business plan innovation. Describe the innovation from the balcony and describe the adaptive and technical challenges within the innovative idea. Analyzing the business plan topic from these strategic levels NOW will help students to have fewer surprises at the end and will increase the value that the business plan brings. With that, apply adaptive and technical thinking, as the development of the business plan moves forward. Look from ALL angles as the worst surprise that can happen to business plan developers is to discover in during the financials section (usually week five and six in the process) that the original plan is unworkable and that they have to start all over at that point. Parenthetically, starting over at this state of plan development is simply not possible if you are bound by a timeline. For anyone who remains curious about adaptive technical this is a quick but very helpful reference sheet: http://www.sgaumc.org/files/files_library/technical_vs_adaptive_challenges.pdf.

Remember, strategic thinking is applied in a variety of venues, from the smallest to the largest. These range from:

- Personal strategies within our own mind "to do better" with action steps included for self-improvement
- Family strategies to create a desired outcome of, for example, settling differences and retaining more contact amongst family members
- Country strategies to improve a process (in the US there is a movement to remove the Electoral College to the Popular Vote. Review this link for more information:

  http://www.nationalpopularvote.com/written-explanation)

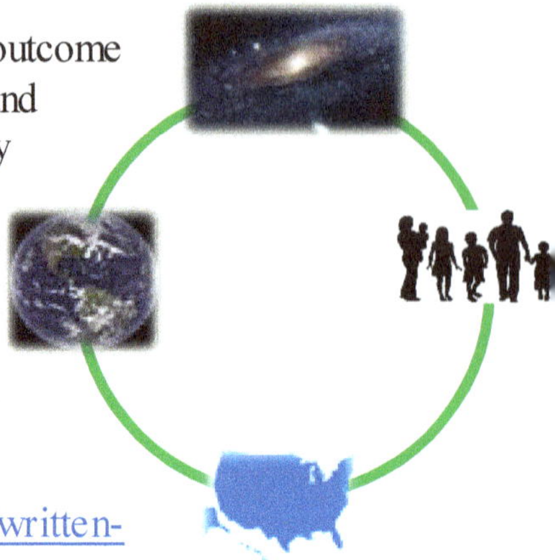

- Country to Country strategies like the Kyoto Protocol (see this link for details: http://unfccc.int/kyoto_protocol/status_of_ratification/items/2613.php)
- And even strategies to explore space (NASA, SpaceX, Boeing, etc.)

Diplomacy is a prime example of strategy. Diplomacy is the connection between people and strategy. A major consideration in diplomacy is ethical ramifications which are considered in the upcoming section below.

Defining an Entrepreneur

It sounds wonderful to be referred to as an entrepreneur. But what does it really mean and can the facets be learned and taught? Nelson (2012) said in his article for Forbes, "I'm pretty sure true entrepreneurship can't be taught. I do hope it can be encouraged." He makes this statement because the willingness to take the financial and emotional risk of potential failure sets the thinker (innovator) apart from the doer (entrepreneur). Here is the article: http://www.forbes.com/sites/brettnelson/2012/06/05/the-real-definition-of-entrepreneur-and-why-it-matters/#25b6cfb171ae. The Merriam Webster online dictionary defines the entrepreneur as "a person who starts a business and is willing to risk loss in order to make money".

The mission of this book is to help everyone who desires to become an entrepreneur. The goal is to help entrepreneurs to mitigate this risk by considering "on the front end" of business plan development all of the "sticky places" that could cause difficulties down the road. The idea is to develop a complete, realistic, and well-thought-out business plan that evaluates and meets said risks with data-driven research and market and industry assessments at the front end rather than find out after production and implementation have started that some of the "land mines" that could be costly or even cause failure down the road were avoidable.

There are many horror stories of start-ups facing unexpected expenses, obstacles, legal issues, etc. that can cripple a new business even before it begins. These failed ideas or "horror stories" of failures are found in the shortcomings of the initial research, analysis, and the "front end" of business planning. Becoming an entrepreneur means that the "unexpected" was predicted through data driven decision making. That way risks were known, understood, faced, and likely eliminated.

Defining Not-for-profit Organization

At this point many ask about what the difference between a for-profit and not-for-profit organization is. The not-for-profit still requires that an organization is financially viable and able to keep the doors open through the creation of revenue. For not-for-profit another term that is often used is "social profit" which means that the surplus funds that are generated are to be designated to improve the world in some specific and predetermined way. Examples are Komen Cancer Research or American Cancer Society, which both operate as 501(c)(3) (not-profit). This means that any money left over after paying operating expenses would be nominated to furthering research and patient care or experience.

While it is true that businesses that are "not-for-profit" / "NPOs" / "nonprofit", are commonly referred to as non-business entities, they still are in need of a sound business plan. Most schools do not allow business plans on non-profit organizations to complete capstone criteria, however. Non-profits often do not pay taxes, but must therefore meet all the other criteria of a non-profit in order to retain the "tax-exempt status". For example, if a non-profit is designed to serve the homeless but non-profit money is spent to educate the director's children, wasted on expensive unnecessary travel, or exorbitant salaries for the director or staff, then the tax-exempt status can be revoked. In California (and tax-exemptions go by the state of a company's headquarters) this tax-exempt status is referred to as the 501(c)(3). There are both, state and federal regulations, that need to be strictly followed. In addition, all expenditures and the salaries of the major employees are part of public record and scrutiny, for that matter.

A good rule is to spend less than twenty percent of the funds collected on administration and eighty percent on serving the target population. For example, Susan G. Komen was in the news for being a non-profit organization that had a charter for cancer research, but they spent a majority of their time and capital (fifty percent) on training the public on breast cancer awareness, while the charter had been formed for research. When an organization moves into the tax-exempt status there are strict and enforceable rules that must be stringently followed.

This is the basics of a not-for-profit. Non-profits are to have a "social profit" or a benefit to a segment of society. These organizations generally have a limited scope and have a very clear set of objectives about how and who they are going to help. Their mission and vision statement is deeply rooted in that cause. Also, for-profit organizations have stockholders and NPOs do not.

This is a short, and certainly incomplete, list of famous "social profit" organizations:

- Bill and Melinda Gates Foundation (the website can be found here: http://www.gatesfoundation.org/)
- Cystic Fibrosis Foundation (the website can be found here: https://www.cff.org/?gclid=CLrkpOPgrtACFcOGaQodF4EF6w)

- Elton John AIDS Foundation (the website can be found here: http://ejaf.org/)
- New York Public Library https://www.nypl.org/support/membership?gclid=CJDq6smd1NACFUSRfgodp-4EMg
- Sanford Burnham Prebys Cancer Discovery Institute http://www.sbpdiscovery.org/Pages/Splash.aspx
- Susan B. Komen Cancer Research
- YMCA (local or national) http://www.ymca.org/ecke

This is a short, and certainly incomplete, list of animal-centered organizations:

- American Anti-Vivisection Society (the website can be found here: http://aavs.org/)
- Hope for Paws (the website can be found here: www.hopeforpaws.org)
- Farm Sanctuary (the website can be found here: http://www.farmsanctuary.org/)
- The Gentle Barn (the website can be found here: http://www.gentlebarn.org/)
- Wildlife Conservation Society

This is a short, and certainly incomplete, list of children-centered organizations:

- Girl Scouts/Boy Scouts (the website can be found here: http://www.gsbadgerland.org/)
- Make a Wish Foundation (the website can be found here: http://wish.org/about-us/our-story
- Hope Foundation for Kids (the website can be found here: http://www.hopefoundationforkids.com/

If readers want to view more non-profit foundations, this is a list of the Top 100 Foundations on the Web: https://topnonprofits.com/lists/best-nonprofits-on-the-web/.

Again, non-profits still have to make enough money to keep the lights on. Many either have a wealthy underwriter (like the Gates Foundation) or the staff has fundraising activities (like Girl Scout cookies) to bring in the operations expenses. Charities and foundations may contact people to donate. However, when considering making a donation, thorough research on the organization is highly advisable as not all of them utilize and spend their funds the same, responsible, and foremost promised way. The mission and vision statement of a non-profit organization are not all that should be considered, but how they spend their received donations is equally important. Research is fairly easy to conduct as all of their records are public.

This is an interesting article on the rules for non-profits: http://lawstreetmedia.com/issues/law-and-politics/non-profit-organizations-rules/.

CHAPTER III - Overview of Business Plan Development

Definition of a Business Plan

A business plan is a step-by-step explanation of how a business is started and how it continues to operate successfully for usually at least five years (this might depend on the audience, the financing authority). There is relevant data that shows a need for the innovation, marketing, operations, financials, and data on target customers and consumers. It is furthermore always an action plan, from start to finish, to help make the product or service a reality. In addition, it presents a detailed analysis of the product or service and strong analytics that show how to build and deliver the innovation. Within the document the financial viability is clear and data-driven. The business plan structures the thoughts and ideas of the entrepreneur and provides a map of the business based on the innovation. Most entrepreneurs have active minds and the business plan format helps to focus their whims and ideas and shape them into an action plan. The business plan also uncovers attends to shortcomings in two ways: 1. A short or undeveloped section of the business plan is a reminder to the entrepreneur that more research and data is needed, 2. After research, a few of the unworkable ideas can be replaced with more dependable alternatives.

Developing an Outline & Understanding its Importance

The outline is the document shell and the skeleton of the business plan as it has all of the twelve (there can be more, if it fits the individual business plan, but there should not be fewer) sections of the business plan in brief but documented and researched format. It helps to catch any holes in the research or analysis early so that the incomplete sections can be noted and show needed efforts to fill in the gaps with more research and analysis.

The better the outline, the more complete and well thought out, the better the whole business plan will be. This step also helps to sort and clarify thoughts and ideas before the true writing begins. The outline is usually approximately ten pages long with about twenty sources, two sources per page. Many entrepreneurs take this outline very seriously and have an outline that is twice that long with much of the detail present they will need for the final business plan. Again, work that is done upfront will not only improve the quality of the business plan, but also save time and hassle later on. And note, the more thorough and complete the outline, the easier it is to fill the sections with meaningful information, data, and their scrutiny.

The business plan is like an onion where more and more layers are added, until the document is well-rounded, concise, and foremost conclusive.

Learning from Fortune 500 Companies

This will section will be helpful as you develop Section 5 of the business plan: Strategic Positioning. It is best to consider two to four different Fortune 500 companies within the industry that the proposed innovation that is going to be offered to analyze business trends and to create a competitive analysis. The goal of this research is to determine the landscape in which the innovation will exist and how to flourish within that space. After all, the Fortune 500 companies have done just that. It will be necessary to dig deep and thoroughly to find out what the companies are really about, not what they write about themselves, but what is actually being done at the "street" level. For example, many companies have glowing reports of their commitment to sustainability on their websites, but through further research it comes to light that those claims are often unfounded (hint: research Apple, Starbucks, and Wal-Mart on this subject matter). With additional research it becomes clear that sustainability efforts that they take credit for are actually performed on the supplier level without any financial investment from the larger company. It is important to determine with data-driven analysis demonstrating that the innovation will bring value to the industry. A list of the current Fortune 500 companies can be found here: http://beta.fortune.com/fortune500.

All research creates data that will help to make better decisions. Often "rabbit trail" research where hours are spent looking and reviewing ideas that did not work at all or that did not work at the time will bring about clear direction for what to do and sometimes more importantly what not to do. The more research that is performed the easier it gets as assessing resources gets more proficient with time as it creates experience. Viability of an idea must be based upon data-driven analysis and will create options or opportunities for the innovation.

This innovation will be thoroughly researched using business sources (more on that later on page 69) and must either be a brand-new idea that will create a new revenue stream for a company or a major process improvement that will create significant cost savings. For the purposes of most business plans, but specifically for academic ones, the expansion of an existing model is not considered an innovation (for example, opening a new Gap store in a different location does not meet the standards and requirements for innovation or for an academic class).

Side note: Student readers of this book who feel they may be using the course as a vehicle to start their own business or develop a product or service that they will pursue in real-life, can go to legal forms (free) and have the instructor and Writing Partner (more on this later on page 78) sign a Nondisclosure Agreement. Furthermore, students have the option to file for Patent Pending (less than $100 and good for one year) to protect their product idea from intellectual theft. Information on US patents can be found here: http://www.uspto.gov/patents-getting-started/patent-basics/types-patent-applications/provisional-application-patent and information on other ways to protect business ideas here: https://www.entrepreneur.com/article/226595. More on patents and patent infringements will be discussed on page 82 concerning global ethics.

Developing a Timeline

The timeline is often developed in Section 9, the "Action Plan". This will provide a time chart that shows all of the action that will be taken to set up the new business. Actions from all sections of the business plan will be included in Section 9, especially from management, marketing, and operations. It is crucial to start and setup realistic and time-driven guidelines to complete the business plan. Individuals who are not successful in writing a business plan usually fall into the trap of not using **SMART** (**S**pecific, **M**easurable, **A**ttainable, **R**elevant, **T**imely) Goals. No matter what previous successes have been, individuals who fall behind or lose focus during the research, analysis, and writing process do fail. Entrepreneurs who take time off during the writing of a business plan find that they often have to start all over again as the research becomes stale and the landscape and opportunities change. Successful entrepreneurs prepare a business plan with all of the focus and direction that is often evident in successful business people. Getting behind in the business plan development endeavors or capstone class, even just a few days, can result in falling so far behind that no recovery is possible and with that the business fails to get off the ground. Business plan writing will require at least twenty hours over the course of eight consecutive weeks. The standards for successful business plans and capstone classes are the highest that most individuals will ever encounter.

Timelines for building a successful business plan need to be clear and measurable. Entrepreneurs should review the following timelines for their needs, to set their own eight-week plan. A suggested timeline for (Brandman University) students looks like this (the weekdays are "no-later-than" and not "set" days):

Monday & Tuesday:	Complete readings as listed in the Syllabus
Tuesday:	1st post to Discussion Board (DB)
Wednesday:	2nd post to DB Start working on the paper/assignment - do the outline as it is "light" work
Thursday:	Start posting responses to other students' DB posts (2 minimum) Continue working on the paper/assignment
Friday:	Check back on the DB and respond to student replies to the students' posts Continue working on the paper/assignment and send it to the assigned writing partner (more on this later on page 78) for feedback and review the writing partner's paper by Saturday (remember, any feedback is helpful and better than no feedback)
Saturday:	Check back on the DB and respond to student responses to the posts Work on the paper/assignment and try to finish it up by the end of the day; look through the feedback received from the writing partner and consider to implement the suggestions
Sunday:	Add finishing touches to the paper, if necessary, and submit it early in case there should be technical difficulties; that way there is enough time to address them; however, be aware that most instructors are not available on Sundays (actually it is best to adopt that they are not available on Saturdays either)

Students at other schools will have to check their syllabus and make adjustments as required and necessary. Once skills are developed for building timelines and following them it will be helpful as the business writer creates the "Action Plan" in Section 10 of the business plan.

Many people wonder why a business plan is often the capstone for fulfilling business degrees. The answer is that the business plan is the ideal document as it gives students an opportunity to demonstrate and apply all they have learned in the MBA program classes. If students are not going to open their own business, this is a great exercise. But if they are planning to open their own business, developing this business plan will give them a strong grasp of the entire system of business, its demands, and requirements. They will be able to understand in a powerful way the entire scope of a business from ideation up onto customer relations and everything in between.

The business plan presents a contextual concept. It is possible that the format that is being used outside of academia is going to be somewhat different from what is found in the classroom. The business plan within this book is built to conform to both academic research, analysis, and writing skills, as well as university and academic standards (this means APA).

In short, the business plan depicted in this book offers students and entrepreneurs the best of both worlds, academia and business. Students will write an academically sound and research-based paper that demonstrates what they have learned in the MBA program and at the same time they will establish practical and clear applications to business. Both, academic and business standards, need to be provided for successful completion of the capstone project. This also makes sense for entrepreneurs because there is no loss, just potential gain, for them to write their business plan according to APA standards. Here is why this does make sense: If the reader of the business plan does not know about academic writing, there is no loss for the writer; if the reader does know APA, he or she will be positively surprised and that might give the entrepreneur an advantage and could mean that one business plan is chosen above another.

A business plan is essential to start a business as it develops all of the key elements of what is necessary to create success. Potential funding usually comes from different sources (more on that in on page 138). The goal is to "use other people's money" when a business is started and the business plan is the document that shows with credibility that the business will bring value and can provide for sustainable growth and profit.

Score.org and SBA.gov are both excellent sources for entrepreneurs, offering templates for financials and information on loans and grants. They both specialize in small businesses and Score provides free advising services to new entrepreneurs; with offices nationwide they offer a great resource for one-on-one help and support. Students are free to inquire as well, however, entrepreneurs take priority and Score might not have the resources available to attend to students at the time.

Applying Relevant APA Considerations for a Business Plan

Writing is an art, but the technical aspects of writing are not, they are a science. For students and entrepreneurs, the "look and feel" of the final business plan is critical. Ragged and inconsistent headings or lack of citations often are interpreted as a lack of scholarship or may even taint the person reading the business plan to think "I wonder if they know what they are writing about". Many good ideas have not come to fruition due to poorly written or hard to read business plans and this is easy to avoid. If the writer of the business plan is not proficient in APA, they can write the plan and then hire a service to make the business plan professional by incorporating APA standards. This is not an option for students as they are required to show that understanding and the application themselves.

At this point most students should know what APA is. After all, the vast majority of schools and classes use APA standards. If there is still need for a refresher look, here is the Owl Purdue site, an excellent source for current APA online guidance: https://owl.english.purdue.edu/owl/resource/560/01/. While it is true that many of the business plans that can be found are not in APA, for academic purposes and to graduate from most Masters programs, it is required that the business plan is in full compliance with the APA (currently 6th edition) standards. This is also true for every assignment business Masters program classes. All assignments will be graded using APA standards as they will make up the business plan document that is required to be written in accordance with APA as well. Entrepreneurs should gain enough knowledge and insight into APA standards to formulate their business plan from that website also. A business plan that uses APA has a fresh and consistent look and will appear to funding sources as being written by someone who has recent business school experience.

There are four major categories that must be adhered to within APA. These are easy to spot when done wrong (yes, the instructor will find these and deduct points if the paper is not following them). They are important pointers for entrepreneurs and good pillars for their business plan. If no other details of the APA standards are applied, the following should be implemented as a minimum: In-Text Citations, APA Headings, and Reference Section. Please do not blame the instructors or comment that they are "too picky", "difficult", "unreasonable", or "cranky" when they insist on holding students to these standards. APA compliance is the foundation of academic standard writing. APA is not a random mechanism to make student lives miserable, but it is a requirement by the university and with that, instructors are just doing their job! A business plan without proper citations and reference section that is unorganized and does not implement proper APA and business writing standards is a bad reflection on the students, their instructors, and a very bad reflection on the university.

Something similar is true for entrepreneurs. The reader of their business plan might consider the lack of proper standard application as a lack of professionalism and seriousness about the endeavor. Even if that might not be the case, a poorly written business plan does not only not explain the innovation well enough, but also reflect badly on the writer him or herself. Either interpretation can be detrimental for getting the innovation financially supported and with that off the ground. Keep in mind, there is a good chance that potential investors will not allow a second submission of a rewritten and improved business plan. One shot is all an entrepreneur might get – make it count, in all aspects; so why not take the time and "do it right".

1. In-text Citations: It is critical in business AND academic writing that proper credit is given to others for their good ideas. Therefore, ALL of the research that is accomplished in developing the business plan needs to be referenced and cited. Here is one of the best references on how to cite in accordance with APA guidelines: https://owl.english.purdue.edu/owl/resource/560/02/.

   These are examples of proper APA citations in accordance with the APA 6th edition:

   According to Young (2000), "Products and services are difficult to develop" (p. 699).

   Bayer (2016) found "products and services are difficult to develop" (p. 199); what complications does this create in developing a business plan?

   Notice there is only one period in each sentence with a citation!

2. APA Headings: Students and entrepreneurs need to pay special attention to the following, headings taken from: http://blog.apastyle.org/.a/6a01157041f4e3970b011570f0dd68970c-popupAPA reference section

APA Style Headings: 6th Edition

Level	Format
1	**Centered, Boldface, Uppercase and Lowercase Heading** Then your paragraph begins below, indented like a regular paragraph.
2	**Flush Left, Boldface, Uppercase, and Lowercase Heading** Then your paragraph begins below, indented like a regular paragraph.
3	**Indented, boldface, lowercase paragraph heading ending with a period.** Your paragraph begins right here, in line with the heading.[a]
4	***Indented, boldface, italicized, lowercase paragraph heading ending with a period.*** Your paragraph begins right here, in line with the heading.
5	*Indented, italicized, lowercase paragraph heading ending with a period.* Your paragraph begins right here, in line with the heading.

[a] For headings at Levels 3–5, the first letter of the first word in the heading is uppercase, and the remaining words are lowercase (except for proper nouns and the first word to follow a colon).

This means that each of the major (twelve) sections of the business plan will be a Level 1 heading (centered and bold faced). Note there is no colon at the end of any of the headings. One core element of the APA requirements is in-text quotes. Here is the rule for those:

APA in-text citations (for long and short quotes):

Long quotes: More than forty words or longer than four lines; these should be used sparingly perhaps one or two within the entire business plan

Short quotes: Usually about eight to ten words

All graphs and pictures must be cited using APA standards as well.

For APA Heading instructions please refer to the Owl Purdue sample paper as they can be difficult to understand without a visual sample and detailed directions: https://owl.english.purdue.edu/owl/resource/560/18/.

3. Reference Section: This is the last section of the business plan (but before appendices, if applicable). The way the sources are listed here depends on the type of source, for example printed (book, magazine, etc.), electronic, and other. As true for all APA standards, the reference section is strict on the formatting requirements and mistakes are easy to spot for the instructor and other readers who are familiar with APA. This means that non-compliance can easily result in loss of points or credibility. For instructions on how to create this part of the business plan refer once again to the Owl Purdue website: https://owl.english.purdue.edu/owl/resource/560/05/.
4. Creating or importing graphs and charts: As mentioned previously it is critical that all business plans contain graphs, charts, tables, and pictures to visualize important parts and information. This is because conception helps understanding what is being explained. It also creates focus points that lead the reader to pay attention to every section. Most A-grade papers have one to three graphs for each of the twelve sections of the business plan. All of these graphs and charts need to be introduced by a short paragraph and wrapped up by another short paragraph after them. This is crucial as documents like a business plan need to, for one, grab the attention of the reader and two, allow to be looked through back and forth.
5. Inserting pictures, graphs, and data: This is what students need to know about inserting graphs financials and maps:
    a. They have to be cited unless they are created by the writer and even then, they need a description underneath. Following this section is an example of how it should be done. Please note, the pictures, graphs, or data sets need to be continuously numbered, as in accordance with APA standards.
    b. Be sure to introduce key concepts in the paragraph above
    c. It has to be explained how they will use the data from the graph below

    Note: All of the graphs and charts in this book have been introduced, cited, and then explained. This is an excellent model to follow for the business plan development.

The following graph depicts the details of using SmartArt. This is an excellent way for students and entrepreneurs to design and develop their own graphs. For anyone who is not familiar with SmartArt, it is a Microsoft program tool, found in Word, PowerPoint, and others that can take a little bit of time to get familiar with. It is therefore important to remember that it does not have to be fancy, but clean and understandable. If further assistance is necessary to work this tool, helpful tips can be found under the "Help" function in Word or online.

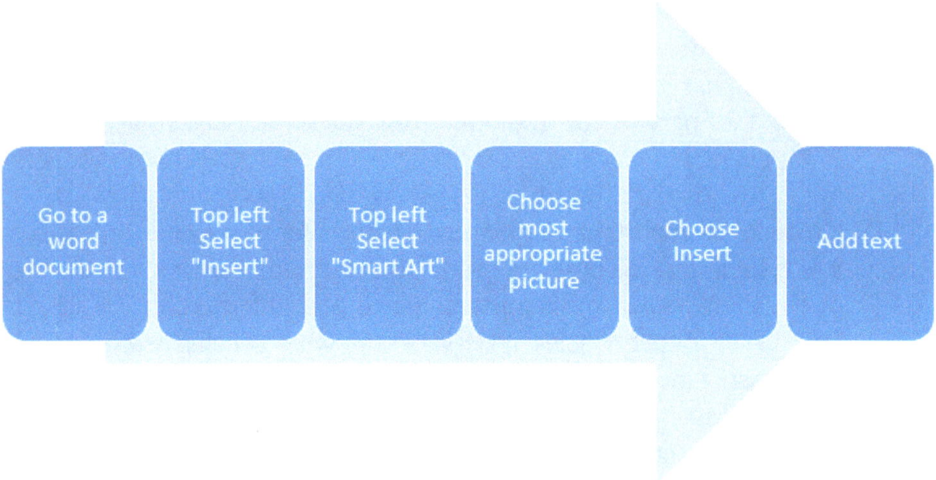

After the text is added, there are many options at the top menu; for example, to include pictures or to change color and/or shape of the SmartArt. Playing around with this in a neutral Word or PowerPoint document (it is not advisable to practice within the assignment or business plan) can be fun and help to improve the looks and usability of the finished SmartArt application.

6. Font Style, Size, & Spacing: Remember the business plan will only use Times New Roman, 12 font size, and will be double spaced. Single spaced documents will not be graded and will receive a zero grade. Note, when the whole document is in final proofreading it is recommended to perform a "global search" to determine that all documents are in Times New Roman 12. That format makes also sense for business plans written by entrepreneurs as it is clean, easy to read, and looks professional. All three of these attributes are something entrepreneurs should always strive for in their business plan presentation.

Utilizing Data-driven Decision Making

The business plan is not a place for opinions. "I really like the Gap and I don't know why they are having so many financial difficulties" or "This xyz company has a female CEO and I have always had great women bosses, so women must be better leaders" are opinions, not facts. The business plan is a place for data-driven decision making and data-driven decision making is comprised of cited research. A valid and good business plan is not based upon opinion or experience. The goal is to have passion for the industry and the innovation, but student and entrepreneur opinions do not constitute data. Data-driven decision making is based upon research and the analysis thereof.

When pronouns are used in the business plan it reads like it is an opinion and not like a data-driven decision making based document. This is why the writer is not to use pronouns such as, "I", "us", "we", "them", etc. In the business plan when the author uses pronouns it is difficult for the reader to understand who the writer is referring to or to relate to the information. The question arises, "Is the "we" the writer and the teacher, or the writer and their roommate, is it a team effort, or somebody entirely else?" Keep in mind, a business plan has to be instantly relatable and understandable for the reader. As a tip, once one section of the paper is completed and ready, do a global search through the search field function and rewrite any section that has a pronoun in it.

Pronouns do not only divert from the professionalism of the business plan, but also the use of pronouns distracts from information and reason why the business plan was written. Pronouns furthermore connote that the writer might be drifting into opinion and out of data driven decision making. The reader's opinion matters, even though the writer's does not when it comes to the business plan. This sounds harsh, however, it goes back to the point that the business plan needs to be written fact based, not opinion based and display data-driven decision making to the reader (who is often the funding source for most business plans).

Data driven decision relies on neutral and relevant data. It is an analysis concerning what the data indicates or predicts. It is powerful when decisions are made based on the researched information and a sound evaluation of it. Students are required to make sure that the data that is being used is not biased, but respectable, current, and from a reliable source (see the source evaluation link on page 69).

A good practice is to use triangulation to evaluate sources. Triangulation of the data means that three separate sources support the same major idea and decisions. For the example of demographics, if a student can show a

.gov source, a local manpower readiness source, and industry trends that support the same idea that would constitute a triangulation for that issue.

Different sources carry different weight, especially .gov and .edu are more entrusted than a .com website and remember, the business plan is not the place for Wiki anything. Therefore, the more profound sources can be provided, the more profound and with that believable and trustworthy the research and evaluation become. The business plan will meet the standards of a business professional in part, depending upon the value of sources used. Keep in mind, if .com sources are used ensure that they are viable and valuable sources.

Knowing Strategy & Structure

As mentioned before, "strategy is a scientific, research based, and analytical look at what currently is and what could be in the future". Strategy is accomplished when an organization from ideation through customer experience works in concert to accomplish a goal. For example, if marketing or operations are not thoroughly versed and "on-board" with strategy, then the strategy will more than likely fail. This means every part of the business needs to contribute and understand its role in making strategy work. In argumentum e contrario, strategy is affected by and affects every part of a business and the business plan.

This section will assist the business plan writer as they develop the "Management Plan", Section 6 of their business plan. Every organization has a structure and this needs to be carefully delineated in the business plan. This is not a "treatise" on leadership, but a management plan for how the roles and responsibilities will be assigned to all personnel. Even if there is only one employee in the company, there needs to be a clear definition of roles and responsibilities. Understanding strategy and structure will also help in Section 4 of the business plan. This is one of the areas in the business plan where as more knowledge of strategy is developed the management plan will improve and vice versa.

There are formal job descriptions with roles and responsibilities and there are organizational charts and the business plan needs both.

The following Organizational Chart can be found at: https://www.google.com/search?q=image+of+an+organizational+chart&tbm=isch&imgil=3dLuC0b7vNzI_M%253A%253B3jltNWVdA9PUgM%253Bhttp%25253A%25252F%25252Fwww.vertex42.com%25252FExcelTemplates%25252Forganizational-chart.html&source=iu&pf=m&fir=3dLuC0b7vNzI_M%253A%252C3jltNWVdA9PUgM%252C_&usg=__gqQryqnZmPv_1m5zZrFtKaMQBS8%3D&biw=1920&bih=971&ved=0ahUKEwj-w-3Axr_OAhUK5WMKHYRSA30QyjcIQQ&ei=9K2vV_75K4rKjwOEpY3oBw#imgrc=3dLuC0b7vNzI_M%3A

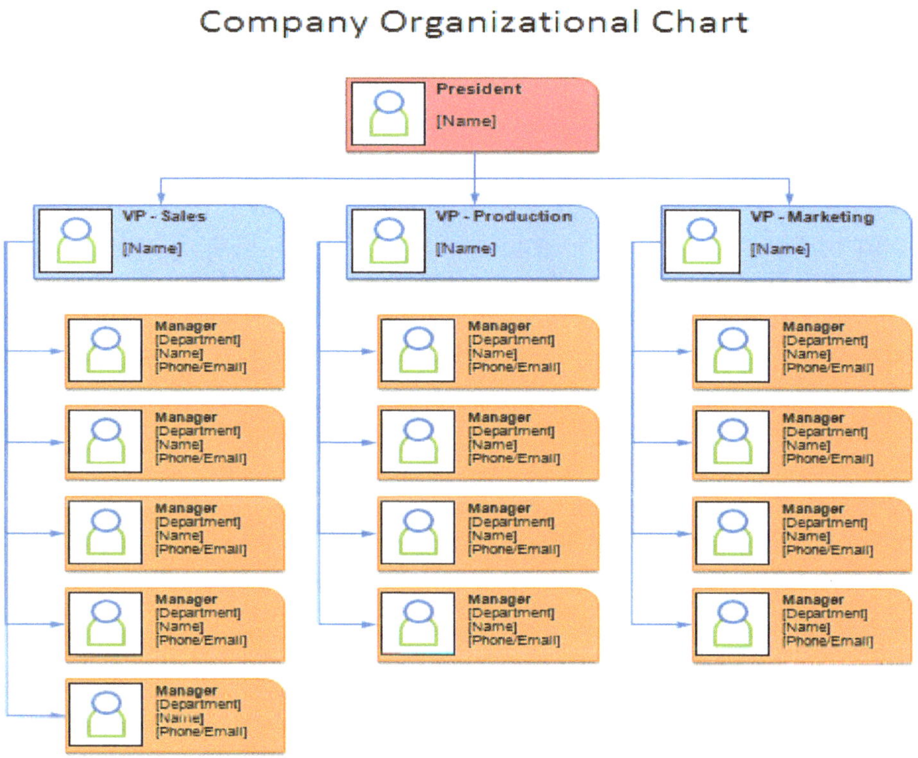

Even though the job descriptions and organizational charts may not be a hundred percent accurate until the business is actually running, it is critical that they are clear, concise, and complete. Companies that have a lack or outdated job descriptions and organization charts often confuse and/or abuse their employees. This is because employees have no document to refer back to when new and different positions are assigned or financial compensation is determined. For a short time, it can be fun to work in an organization where "all hands are on deck" but over time that freedom often creates less effectiveness and efficiencies. Sometimes "Jacks of all trades"

in business are very useful in the beginning but over time they can slow the business down. Also the "Jack of all trades" employee is often ill prepared to move up or to move to another company as they become or are considered (perhaps wrongfully so) "a master of none of the critical skills in business" or a "know it all".

However, even with the best of job descriptions, it is only what is on paper and may not resemble "how business actually gets accomplished". One of the ways that Dr. Eckmann as a consultant has been able to see "how an organization really works" is by attending social functions, office luncheons, or watching "down time" in the office where the CEO and his or her direct reports are also in attendance. This can be as the CEO goes into or out of the business, who they speak to and who they smile at; notice who they call when things go right and who they call when things go wrong (these are usually different people).

Becoming a better observer of what is actually happening (sometimes using balcony and dancefloor skills) helps to be quite adept at seeing what is really going on in organizations (as a consultant, business plan writer, or employee). It is often obviously clear which of the direct reports has the most favor by watching the CEO (which direct report gets the most time and attention; which direct report gets "kudos" for their ideas from the CEO). From experience, watching an organization gives a much clearer picture than any organizational chart. However, once again, after the discrepancies are uncovered in the organizational chart it is efficient to as soon as possible get things on paper to resemble the actual work flow. Discrepancies between "actual" and "what is supposed to be" is often the places where the work slows down and blame becomes a common practice.

Use any previous experience in business as the business plan is developed. Try to avoid some of the mistakes that may already have been witnessed in professional environments. Think about the differences in "proposed and actual" structures in places of work. Notice who appears to have the "hot hand" and who seems to be "kicked to the curb" when ideas, opportunities, and solutions are being offered. Observe who is looked to for innovative ideas and who is not. Favoritism abounds and it is wise to know the actual organizational chart, but it is even wiser to observe how business actually gets done. Practiced observation and reflection will expose truths that are not visible on paper. Draw on previous experiences (good and bad) as a way to design the business plan with clear roles and responsibilities.

Also, consider each organization will be unique depending upon the industry and the innovation. Some within the organizations are very "sales driven". This means that the person closest to the CEO would probably be the VP of Marketing or Sales. Other organizations are very engineering driven, like Raytheon, Boeing, and Northrop Grumman, as most of their products and services are sold by those organizations that are derived from the engineering teams. An array of organizations is driven by the supply chain. The VP of Supply Chain is usually at the "right hand" of the CEO and many of the innovations and most of the process improvements in the organization come from the supply chain. Lastly, many organizations are run by the Finance VP. He or she has the final say; so for all projects and many of the considerations, opportunities, and threats are assessed through that department. So as the organizational chart is developed consider all of these issues.

Likewise deliberate the typical organizational chart for the industry of the innovation. Some industries are more likely to be driven by finance (banks, savings, and loans, for example). Others are more likely to be ambitious about marketing like many technology companies. There are always anomalies to be found in industries, like a technology companies that are very risk averse or a bank that is very customer-centric. It has been our experience that many companies resemble the fears and pride of their CEOs. So if the CEO is risk averse so will the organization be; if the CEO is highly innovative then the organization will be more innovative as well (but may not make as many strong financial decisions).

The physical location of "who sits where" is also very important and there needs to be a description of the physical plant in the management plan. The person on the right hand of the CEO is generally considered the "right hand" and known to have more power than the person on the left. The person who is furthest away from the CEO or on a different floor is perceived as having less power. Those who are in "cubes" are perceived as having less power than those with offices. Interoffice location is a great interoffice power indicator. Connecting the management plan to the physical plant is essential. Within the operations plan will need to be a description of how the product or service will be developed and what that physical plant layout would be.

Also consider that there are organizational charts for departments, not just the entire company. This is an example of a supply chain organizational chart which could be developed for Section 8 of the business plan. This is an example of a very large organization supply chain structure from: https://www.google.com/search?q=organizational+chart+for+a+supply+chain&tbm=isch&tbo=u&source=univ&sa=X&ved=0ahUKEwj73LTQyb_OAhVC0WMKHfpuCVoQ7AkINA&biw=1920&bih=971#imgrc=-LSaSsUbvPEaFM%3A:

The operations plan will enclose the description of how the product or service will be developed and what that physical plant layout will look like.

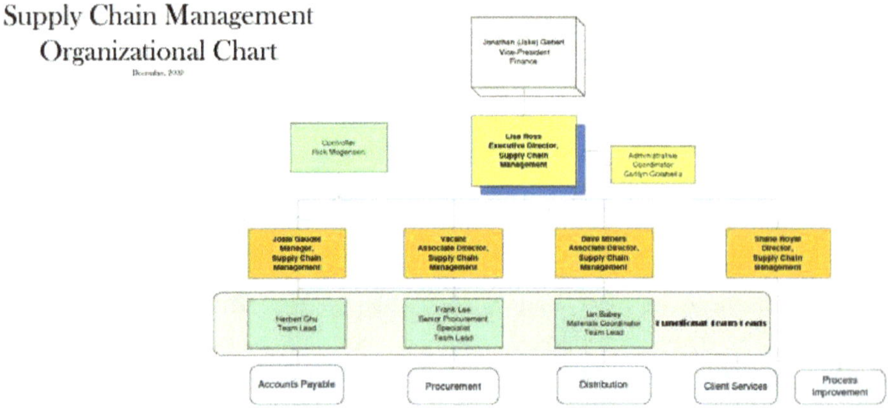

This information will be covered in Section 8 of the Business Plan and will require a process flow map.

After considering this section on strategy and structure think about how "structure" will find a place in the innovation's business plan: What department will be central to success (there will be only one)? The organization needs to be designed in accordance to what has been learned about the industry of the innovation and what the data-driven decision making leads them to analyze what will work best.

Business plan authors should build an organizational chart and process flow maps for the innovation and consider all that has been learned about strategy and structure; consider what needs to be accomplishes and what the best way to get there is. Tie strategy and structure to purpose, mission, and vision.

This section will assist the business plan writer as they develop Section 4 of the business plan. Strategy is developed starting from the balcony view of the recognized opportunity. This means that strategy starts with the big picture and moves to the "dancefloor" of identifiable and discrete action plan steps. A business plan starts with the knowledge of the resources and talent that is currently available, the industry, what the demographics are of the intended customer or customers. Then starts researching what is needed to fill in all that is necessary that is not at hand. Strategy is developed with a lot of thinking, question asking, and then researching to find the answers to all pertinent questions. Often as research is conduced, even more questions pop up to research further and eventually to answer. This is a great time to solicit input from other people, the writing partner(s), and others who may be familiar with marketing, operations, the industry that is being considered or any others who will listen and give feedback. For students, conversations with the writing partner, who is very familiar with course requirements, will be very helpful no matter whose business plan is discussed. This is the phase to brainstorm with other people, students, peers, family, friends, and even possibly the instructor and if possible investors or financing authorities.

One of the most popular analysis for process improvement is referred to as DMAIC. **DMAIC** stands for **D**efine, **M**easure, **A**nalyze, **I**mprove and **C**ontrol. This will be applied to Section 8 of the Business Plan, "Operations". Below is a graph with some of the components of DMAIC:

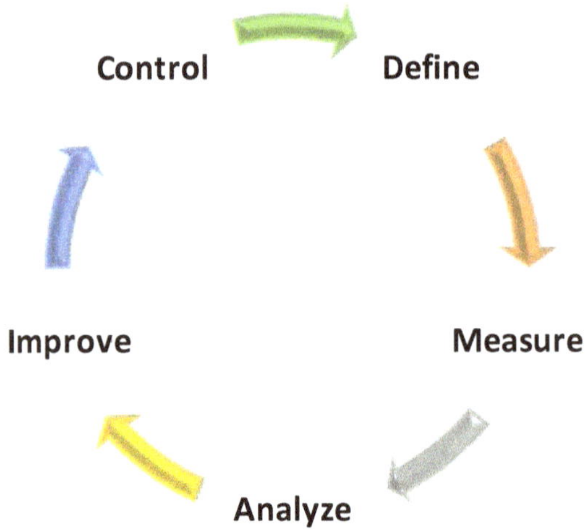

Define: Innovation, business, structure, plans, identify problems, etc.

Measure: Time, production, delivery, cost, controls, set targets, etc.

Analyze: What, how, when, who, process mapping, risks, inefficiencies, etc.

Improve: Business processes, generate new ideas, etc.

Control: Quality, improvement measures, etc.

Any improvement plan must be as unique as the innovation and company are. The most important part is the analysis of the current status and the comparison to the envisioned and desired state. Discrepancies can be found easily during this process. This creates a simple equation: Desired state minus status quo equals the need for improvement and change. The application of process improvement is much more difficult in reality, but is easy to visualize as a concept in the below seen way, based on the above mentioned concepts.

This graphic with description were taken from Kerstin Young's business plan for her MBA program.

Figure 15: The illustration shows how simple the concept of process improvement is, while the implications in reality might be much more difficult. Note: From Creative Commons

Creating a Quantifiable Revenue Stream

Information from this section will be helpful for developing Section 9 of the business plan. For this business plan students and entrepreneurs alike will need to show that their innovation, product, or service (or product and service) will create an additional revenue stream and add value. A revenue stream is a new source of income. It is not sufficient for an academic business plan to just create "good will" or to improve a brand. The value from revenue needs to show a positive trend (revenue over total expenses). This value and revenue need to be based upon business research and occur over three to five consecutive years and profit needs to be at least $30,000 in the first year. For an entrepreneurial business plan the revenue expectation might be somewhat different and greatly depends on the innovation and the funding demand. However, the vast majority of them require to show for a profound revenue stream in order for investors to even be interested. Most investors (banks, family, SBA, etc.) are going to want to see a positive revenue stream that is based upon data-driven decision making. This is a most critical part of the business plan, as any investor wants to know that they will receive a return on their investment (ROI).

A valuable source to consult on revenue stream can be found here: http://gsvc.org/wp-content/uploads/2014/01/Revenue-Streams_Business-Model-Generation.pdf.

Reminder: If the above source, or any other source, is used in the business plan, it needs to be cited and referenced. For easier accessibility it is advised to save the document or any other document that is used to the desktop.

Consideration of Ethical Ramifications of a Business Plan

Ethics is a very important topic in life and in business as it connects to underlying values. They are usually a consideration in the mission and vision as well as the management and operations plan sections of the business plan. The topic of ethics has been discussed and written about for the past 2,500 years, starting with Aristotle, Moses, and Sunzi, aka Sun Tzu. "The wise who are trained and disciplined shine out like beacon-lights. They earn money just as a bee gathers honey without harming the flowers. And they let it grow as an ant-hill slowly gains in heights. With wealth wisely gained they use it for the benefit of all" (Digha Nikaya n.d.). Now it is feasible to ask, "how many wise are there?", "are we wise?", "do we support only the wise?", and "what do we do to promote wisdom?".

Kenneth Blanchard and Norman Vincent Peale came up with a quick ethics test. Students are encouraged to take this and see what they think: http://www.au.af.mil/au/awc/awcgate/sba/ethics.htm

1. It is legal?
2. Is it balanced and fair?
3. If your action was to be put on the front page of the newspaper tomorrow, how would you feel?

The three questions above can be used in a variety of ways and applied in both personal and professional settings. For the business plan operations section the ethical plans for sourcing, manufacturing, worker safety and health, packaging, and customer service are all critical. As in the management plan, the operations plan has many ethical considerations.

Ethics today is even more complicated and with consumers able to research companies in detail, nothing can be assumed to be hidden. Even emails that are assumed to be private can and do "leak" out for everybody to see. In the world today there cannot be any assumption of privacy. There are cameras everywhere, even drones, for better or worse. You can be spending dinner time with family at your beach home and have a small drone fly about four feet over your heads. Privacy and discretion are becoming more and more an illusion. Which means that what used to be done in private is now public information both personally and professionally.

The ethics perspective impacts how we organize our businesses. Some companies are very focused on ethics and run ethical businesses from strategy to consumer interface and sustainability. Other companies pretend to be ethical and have all of the standards but do not pursue them in practice. Then there are companies that do not have any ethical strategies as a focus. Below is a link of the most ethical businesses worldwide. The awardees were from 131 companies from 21 countries, representing 45 industries. The list includes fourteen 10-time honorees and thirteen first-time honorees: http://www.forbes.com/sites/karstenstrauss/2016/03/09/the-worlds-most-ethical-companies-2016/#49daa5f773dc. This ratio is very hopeful that ethical standards are very important yesterday, today, and tomorrow.

Many people are confused as to what is ethical, what is moral, and what is right. Some people and organizations find the debate too difficult so they do nothing at all to participate in it and hence do nothing to implement any of those fail safes - not a great solution. Some things are simply right or wrong, like taking advantage of little children, the weak, the helpless or feeble. Other things are harder to assess, like employee satisfaction.

The below outlined ethical considerations would be included in the supply chain or operations section as these primarily apply to Section 8. Please review the Big Dozen questions below on ethical products and services and address each in the business plan. The list below was developed by Dr. Eckmann. Notice that some consumers, and a growing number of them, will choose to pay more rather than buy products that do not meet the following standards:

1. Are children being exploited to build or maintain the product or service?
2. Are the people building the product or service being paid a fair and legal wage or are they being exploited?
3. Are there methods for employees to gain redress without retaliation?
4. Is the workplace safe and free from hazardous materials and/or circumstances?
5. Are the processes used to develop the product unnecessarily challenging for environment and natural resources (fresh water, air, earth, oceans)?
6. Are scarce or critical resources exhausted in the making of the product or service? (More on this in the following link: https://www.reference.com/science/examples-scarce-resources-6be4ade2d2cd2df9)
7. Is the impact of the manufacturing, transportation, etc. as sustainable as possible?
8. Does the product or service work as advertised?
9. Is there adequate customer service and redress?
10. Does the product or service have a long-term sustainable model?
11. Is there fair hiring practices?
12. Does the CEO make too much money? How does overpaying the CEO affect the profitability of the organization? (More on this in the following link: https://www.thestreet.com/story/13045780/1/the-10-most-overpaid-ceos-running-multi-billion-dollar-companies.html)

Keep in mind, often times the understanding of ethical concerns requires ethical awareness, which not everybody has. Ethical standards and their applications can and do differ from person to person. It is interesting to note that ethical awareness and change are frequently triggered by other people questioning the status quo and even criticizing others for their lack thereof. With that in mind, do not shy away from discussing ethical ramifications and describing the reasoning for the chosen ethical standards in the business plan.

Understanding Legal & Structural Issues

This is often considered when writing the "Management Plan", Section 6 and "Operations Plan", Section 7. Every business and every part of a business has legal and structural concerns. As mentioned previously, when staff is hired there are legal restrictions and requirements for pay, unemployment insurance, and a host of other laws that need to be followed (allowing breaks, offer break rooms, etc.). If there is manufacturing to be completed, if some of the parts in the supply chain are assembled or sub-assembled outside of the US or even if it crosses borders, then there are laws that apply as well.

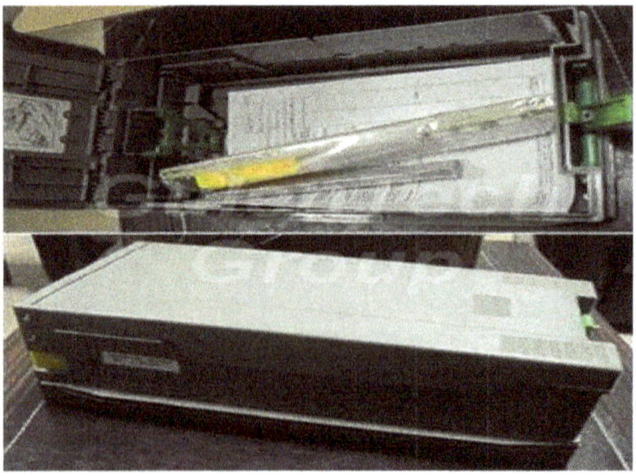

Many manufactured items have smaller sub-assembly parts that can create a problem. For example, one aspiring entrepreneur attempted a business plan for a new ATM that would feature "live" talk with a call center so that people in front of an ATM could get questions answered by banking personnel. ATMs have thousands of moving parts and sub-assembly components (cameras, electronics, encasements, etc.) as seen in the pictures:

https://www.google.com/search?q=what+are+the+sub+assembly+parts+for+an+ATM&tbm=isch&tbo=u&source=univ&sa=X&ved=0ahUKEwjY3YH6vcbOAhUN22MKHW_YD-0QsAQIOw&biw=1920&bih=971#imgrc=YWL-yhJGLLmgVM%3A

So this means that each of the laws and each of the components of the ATM would need to be known so that any structural or legal issues could be addressed early. With that, the entire business plan could fail if one of the key suppliers or elements of the ATM were found to be out of compliance with the law.

A well thought-out business plan displays a clear understanding of some of the subtler things that can go wrong and these possible structural issues are researched and mitigated as much as possible. This also translates that structural issues can come in all shapes and forms. Below is a list of some (not even close to all) things to consider for the "Operations Plan", Section 8 of the business plan. Read carefully and think what might apply (and what else might apply) to the innovation under consideration:

1. What are the sourcing issues? Are there legal constraints that are in place now or are proposed that could change the viability of a business plan?
2. What are the sub-assembly concerns and/or present or future legal restrictions?
3. Are the terms and conditions of all contracts with suppliers legal and enforceable?
4. What is the best and cheapest transportation and will that meet the needs of the customer about receiving products within a desirable timeframe?
5. What are the inventory concerns? What is the shelf life for the product? What is the cost to store (keep in mind that storage needs to be insured as well, which is a cost)? Is there storage available?
6. Are their concerns with the Better Business Bureau that need to be addressed in the industry for the innovation?
7. What are the standards for warranty in the industry and what does that cost?

Applying Life Cycles & Stages

This part will assist in writing Section 5, "Product and Service". Life cycle is an interesting topic that can apply to innovations, individual people, or to particular industries (to name a few). Considering the life cycle of the industry and the innovation is an intelligent way to consider the innovation in context. A life cycle is a series of often predictable stages that an innovation, individual, group, resource, or industry passes through. Typically, there is a chart like the one below:

Infant Stage	Teenage Stage	Middle Adult Stage	Old Stage
This is described as a time where the subject under review is just beginning hallmarks are: can't support itself, needs lots of assistance, is highly unique and is often difficult to deal with.	**This is described as a time where the subject under review is starting to make independent decisions, but still can't quite support itself. Often difficult to deal with.**	**This is described as a time where financial security is at hand. Makes independent decisions, but often is critical of those in the infant or teenage stage as they are a financial drain.**	**This is described as a time where financial security is assured. Makes independent decisions, has difficulty coming up with innovation and change. Some want things to stay as they are.**
Example People: Babies need a lot of assistance, often react to the same stimulus differently. Take a lot of time and patience.	**Example People:** Start to want to make own decisions but still wants Middle and Old State people to support their ideas. A time of great creativity.	**Example People:** Have money in the bank. Have success, does not often come up with innovative ideas. Begin to say things "this is the way it was for me." Tends to have more patience with the Infant Stage.	**Example People:** Has money in the bank. Resists change. Tends to get along with the Teenage Stage as they begin to value their innovative ideas. May have some fear of the future.
Example Organization: Just starting the innovation. Borrows money	**Example Organization:** Has had little success yet. Full of great ideas.	**Example Organization:** Has had more successes and failures.	**Example Organization:** Needs to reinvent itself but often lacks

from bank or parent company. Has lots of ideas, but often lacks processes that work.	Often somewhat angry that others don't value their ideas or what they are doing.	Lacking many new ideas. Has money in the bank. Values having money in the bank.	ideas on how to do that. Often has money in the bank, but sees the trend lines heading southward.
Example Writing: Start with a draft, lots of ideas, does not seem to be clear to anyone other than the writer. Often confusing and highly unique.	**Example Writing:** Moves some ideas into outline form, many stops and starts, very unhappy with criticism, ideas are still forming, lots of contradictions but starting to take shape.	**Example Writing:** A draft is prepared of the writing. The draft has form and a beginning, middle and end. The subject has been researched not much new information is being added.	**Example Writing:** A final is prepared. This is either submitted to the instructor or to the publisher. The idea is completed. Often some depression after the writing is done and fears for future subjects for writing.

After reviewing the above information on stage theory consider which stage the proposed innovation is in, what stage the industry is in, and what stage of development is the organization in that is funding the innovation. If the funding source is "old age" and the innovation is in the "teenage stage", what possible options are there for strategies for mitigations that can be employed? A suggestion would be, if the funding source is "old age stage" and the innovation is in the "teenage stage", it would be critical to include "old age" language in parts of the business plan, especially the financial section. If there is a significant disconnect between the writer's demographic of the business plan and the funding source, it is important to "build a bridge" so that funders will understand the overall business plan (funding does not follow doubt or confusion).

Prepare a life cycle of the innovation and the company and include this document into the business plan. The more writers of business plans think about life cycle on a personal and professional level the more they will be able to create successful strategies. This is most often a graphic or visual in the business plan.

CHAPTER IV - Overview of Professional Business Learning, Reading, & Writing

It is indispensable for a successful business plan to develop flow, tone (voice), and focus through professional business writing. There are many different strategies that need to be used in order to accomplish that goal. This section will address the most important ones.

Having another set of eyes on the business plan is a great way of improving such an important document. The idea of employing a writing partner will be explored throughout the book and is worth mentioning again in this section as writing partners can greatly help with professionalism in writing as long as he or she is proficient in it.

Check the entire business plan for the following and address them accordingly:

- Every section needs to be about the innovation within the section's topic
- Introductions at the beginning of each major section and concluding paragraphs at the end of each major section
- Do not use pronouns and stay true to how the audience is addressed
- Avoid long sentences and take out sentences that are confusing or do not support the basic idea
- Read the paper out loud; sometimes business plan writers overlook certain poor aspects, but detect them when they are heard
- Have an outsider read the paper and have them make remarks and give input/feedback
- Ensure that no new ideas or unrelated ideas are presented that belong somewhere else in the business plan
- Understand that the sections of the business each discuss a different aspect, but still need to fit one document (the business plan)
- Take out all of the cliché like "on the other hand" or "it is what it is" or "and so it seems like" or "at the end of the day."
- Take out slang or abbreviated words like "my bad", "what's up", or "dope."

Take out jargon or acronyms unless the audience for the funding source is very familiar with the terms and keep in mind that this might be difficult to assess. For example, "MRE" is used in the military to mean "Meals Ready to Eat". If the military is the funding source then MRE could be used, but if not, do not use it. If acronyms are used, be sure to introduce them even if one of the sources for funding might be familiar with them. Many acronyms have multiple meanings in different contexts, so avoid them or use them with extreme care. For example, "ROE" in business means "Return On Equity", while in the military it means "Rules of Engagement". Here is a great source for acronyms and to check of they have multiple meanings: http://www.acronymfinder.com/.

Understanding the Importance of Starting with a Literature Review

A literature review is a list and description of significant business and academic sources that are relevant to the subject under review and the writer plans on using. The literature review is more than just a summary of germane data; it is a critical analysis of each source, providing an overview of the subject under review.

Among other things, the literature review will help students and entrepreneurs to be able to know if their innovation is truly a fresh and new idea. For example, someone wanted to develop a product to sell on Amazon but once research commenced it was discovered that there were already five companies selling similar products and that the idea was not new, hence not an innovation. That makes the literature review in part a tool to prove that the innovation is not just a duplication of something already offered in the marketplace. Developing something that already exists would be fraud with infringement and copyright violations and thus would not qualify for a successful business plan innovation.

Remember, starting the literature review it is a bit like learning to swim. It does not work without getting in the water and getting wet. One has jump in and thrash around before one can become proficient. The same is true for the literature review. Students have to just begin even though it might not be clear yet what the innovation (product or service) will exactly be and that leaves all other questions open as well. BUT at this stage of the business plan, this is okay. With research students and entrepreneurs will find out many things. One may be that the original idea will not work and that they need to come up with another plan; another takeaway that may be learned is that there is insufficient data to proceed with the initial idea and direction.

It is not uncommon for someone to think about an idea for years and to ruminate about how successful the business idea could be. Writing a literature review is a fruitful way to begin determining if there is viability in the idea. Doubts can be eliminated either way.

Sometimes it is found that the innovation is a good idea, but there is no customer base to support the innovation (at least not in the envisioned location), or that the cost of manufacturing or distribution is too high. All of this will only become apparent with research. With that, beginning the literature review without knowing exactly how it will all turn out is necessary. With research the waters will clear.

Students have a lifeguard on duty in form of their instructor and the discussion board is also a great tool to post and seek answers for key questions so that all of the students can learn at the same time. Entrepreneurs also need to find a forum. Friends, family members, associates, former peers or instructor, or anybody who will review and make comments on the working business plan can provide the feedback they seek.

Even though that the struggle can be very real, it is common that those building a business feel somewhat isolated and alone and thus it is helpful if they have someone to turn to for advice, who is trustworthy. If there is any doubt, a NDA (Non-Disclosure Agreement) can be downloaded and signed for free off of the Internet; see the following link for further information: http://www.forbes.com/sites/allbusiness/2016/03/10/the-key-elements-of-non-disclosure-agreements/#3af8980c411b). Feeling overwhelmed at this stage is not abnormal and can even be expected and should therefore be anticipated and even embraced as it means that there are many ideas that can find application. Often a great struggle is a precursor to a very impressive business plan.

As the business plan is used for a capstone class, the literature review is a process that gives examples of relevant data that would show a business case for the viability of the business idea. The literature review is essential as business plan writers need to show that they have the ability to accomplish thorough and organized business and data research and the same research is the foundation for the business plan.

Utilizing Library Sources

At this point please remember that Google research is often not sufficient, not reliable, and not fact based research. The information found on the Internet is sometimes undependable and biased. Scholarly sources are still frequently not found or accessible online. The links for them can be tracked down online, however, some sources still have to be accessed through libraries or schools. Entrepreneurs would want to include articles from the library (peer reviewed) and current information found from sites/magazines/newspapers like Bloomberg, Forbes, the Wall Street Journal, the New York Times, Harvard Business Review, Wired, Fast Company, and other reputable business journals. WIKIs must not be used as a source in a business plan or any academic environment (one does not need to go to business school to learn how to Google, nor will businesses and employers expect business school graduates to use Google as a resource source; they could do that on their own).

The U.S. Library System offers a variety of services, but also more than just books; they offer English classes as well. They further provide a list of public libraries across the country, allow to have books and other materials shipped from other locations to the closest library for free, and provide online access services for research materials. The following link is to access their main site: https://www.usa.gov/libraries.

Defining Research Relevance

It is critical that all research presented in the business plan is relevant and therefore current (anything older than five years is usually too old, except for census data). Literature reviews should have three to four sections of individualized research, which can and should be divided by section headers for clarity and better understanding. The research would be equally distributed among the three to four sections (sections that will be found in the business plan, like marketing, demographics, the industry in which the product or service falls, etc.).

Entrepreneurs need to include researched data on the location that they plan to start their business in, the potential customer base (demographics, usually using a .gov source), operations, suppliers, and the industry for the innovation. Research cannot (for students) and should not (for entrepreneurs) be repeated (reused) in a different sections of the business plan. This means that if a source is used in, for example, the management section, that same source cannot be used again in the financial section. Therefore, it must be chosen wisely where the sources will best fit and with that be best utilized. It is common that not all of the sources presented in the literature review find use in the final business plan. This is because the literature review is created very early in the business plan development process and the project stage and the writers may find better or different sources that are more relevant as they continue their research and are starting to better understand the product or service. The literature review is a great place to get a feel for and analyze the landscape for the new business venture.

It is important to point out that some information for the literature review might be difficult to be found. It often takes hours to find only one suitable source. The more data is gathered on the front end of the business plan the better. Keeping track of where every source is found from the beginning is crucial as researchers will probably not be able to find it again once they move on. The more organized business plan writers are in the beginning of the research process, the better. It is a good and helpful idea to create subfolders under "Favorites" on the computer and to save noteworthy websites there. The more difficult a source is to find the more valuable it probably is. This means that the source is not readily available to competition and may contain critical information to provide a distinction for a new business. Also, as students sign on to the school libraries it is hard to bring up the sources just by the link as the login through the school website is different from the login through the article's homepage link.

A good way to ensure accessibility to the file is printing the document to PDF and save the growing list of sources it in a designated folder on the computer. Again, to create folder and subfolders to save documents and websites helps to organize them and grants easier access later on. Always notate the sources immediately and in APA format, so that there is no risk of not finding it again (Murphy's Law). Work that is done right away and correctly is work that will not have to be done later on or repeatedly. Library staff is always very helpful. That is what they are there for and they take great pride in "digging" up the most difficult to find information possible. For Brandman students the Chapman Library can be accessed from www.my.Brandman.edu.

To evaluate sources correctly is utterly crucial. Here is a good source on how to assess a business source accurately: https://owl.english.purdue.edu/owl/resource/553/01/. Additional information for Brandman students is found in Course Information under "Literature Review". Students of other schools can inquire with their instructor. If there is still a need for more help, review this one-page document: http://guides.library.ucsc.edu/write-a-literature-review.

Creating Business Research

Business research is the cited (in accordance with the APA standards) research on other businesses, potential partnerships, competitors, suppliers, regulations, legal and other restrictions, customers, and any other needed areas of the business plan. These sources form the business rationale for the success of the business plan. The information is often found by researching the names of individual companies. Finding individual companies in the industry that the innovation and business will be operating in is already part of research. Understanding the industry and environment is truly step one of the research and means understanding the scope of the innovation process.

Please remember to keep a list of these sources and the links that were used, categorizing them by using the APA subheadings of the business plan, so that they can be found again later on. It is the bane of many business plan writers when they cannot find the source information for a critical underpinning for the business plan. It helps to create a separate document of all the research using the subheadings of the business plan. For example, all sources for the management section would go under that heading and all sources for operations would go under that heading. These sources will form the literature reviews the competitive analysis, the action plan, as well as all other data-driven analysis. It is helpful to look for both, positive and negative publicity, and legal cases like lawsuits as this will establish the need for the product or innovation.

Entrepreneurs will use business terminology and language in their business plan. It is crucial to only use words that they know the meaning of. Business vocabulary will expand as research is completed and will become easier and more natural to use. For students it is important to show that they know how to use and apply the words that they have learned in their business program. For example, do not use "cash" when talking about "revenue stream" or do not use "flow or steps" when the topic is "supply chain". Furthermore, do not use cliché ("At the end of the day", etc.) and do not use slang ("totally", "really", "awesome", etc.) as there are always better words for both. A good place to start looking for business terminology is in the glossary section of the textbooks of the core business classes. For entrepreneurs the best place to start might be the internet; just use search engines to look for "business terms".

Understanding Academic Integrity

Academic integrity is a professional and business requirement. Academic integrity applies inside and outside of the classroom. Even a small lapse in citing the work of others can cause the reader of a business plan to question the veracity of the author, the business plan itself, and even the innovation. The more ethical standards that are applied and deference that is given to academic integrity, the more likely the business plan will be given a thoughtful look by the serious investor. The academic integrity policy from Brandman University resembles other accredited universities'. Entrepreneurs should also have equivalent scholarship integrity standards. Any business plan that fails to acknowledge and attribute the work of others will, at some point, lose credibility if not funding. The policy in its entirety can be found under "Academic Integrity Policy" in the current Brandman University Catalog at: https://www.brandman.edu/files/documents/academic-catalog-programs/2016-2017_Catalog_6_24_16_0.pdf. The policy covers the following major points:

1. Business plan authors must submit only their own work (buying or borrowing work is a violation)
2. Business plan authors must cite (using APA) ALL of the work of others they do **utilize or present** as they must give credit to others appropriately
3. Students must not "cut and paste" **from their own previous work - the only exception is the students' own assignments <u>from the current class</u>, as they build on one another; so, previous work from earlier assignments <u>from the current class</u> can be used and submitted with the final assignment without having to cite it, but not work from previous classes** (this is because it is not possible to cite work from previous classes properly)
4. Business plan authors must not "cut and paste" other people's (people they know or do not know) papers from discussion boards or assignments (current or past); this also applies to classroom discussion boards

Students can fail the assignment or the entire class for any of all of the above infractions or any lack of academic integrity. Stealing anyone else's ideas is called a violation of Intellectual Property laws and is not only ethically wrong, it is illegal, in and outside of the classroom.

For students, when the final project is submitted, the paper will receive a score for academic integrity violations. If the score is too high, then the paper is failed without any opportunity for resubmission. This is what the TurnItIn program does (students will submit their work through this program). It automatically searches the document for academic integrity violations, grades the number of violations, and assigns a score. The score holds a threshold over which the student fails the assignment and potentially the entire class. The consequences are outside of the student's and teacher's/instructor's influence as the program cannot be circumvented, disabled, or adjusted. Here is a good source pertaining to US copyright information, explaining what intellectual property is and how violations can occur and are punished: http://www.copyright.gov/about/.

Comparing the Differences of Describing & Applying

For the business plan it is important that all data be applied to the chosen innovation. A business plan is not a "teaching document", but a document that shows how, where, and when business concepts will be put to work with the innovation. This means that the purpose of the business plan is not to teach (describing or defining) about the concepts within the business plan, but to show how business concepts do apply (or will be used). For students using the concepts from the textbooks, they should be applying them throughout the entire business plan. A sign of business or professional communication is demonstrated by speaking or writing about how notions apply rather than defining or describing the business concepts. Stating definitions is usually considered rudimentary and not professional. Below are side-by-side examples of applications versus descriptions. Remember conceptual application is the heart of a business plan:

Defining (not to be used in Business Plan)	Applying (is to be used in Business Plan)
"Supply chain is described as . . .."	"The supply chain that entails . . . is applied in this project in the following three ways . . .."
"Demographics are used to identify the target customer."	"The target demographics of race, religion, and gender for the product are . . .."
"Management is a process of how people are organized to accomplish their jobs."	"The organizational chart will drive the management plan in the following three ways: . . .."
"An action plan is a set of steps required to complete a business plan."	"The following 15-step action plan will describe all necessary functions that will be needed to be accomplished in the next 30 days. These steps are inclusive of all of the sections of the business plan including marketing, management, operations, and financial."

Remember paraphrasing is still not applying the definition. Applications almost always have concrete examples of business steps necessary to accomplish something. Any time definitions are included in a business plan it is frankly wasted space and is considered filler material, text with little to no value, at least to the business plan and its reader. In a business plan pictures, graphs, charts, and tables (like the one above) are always stronger than definitions.

The only time a definition might be required is if a used term is specific to the industry or the innovation and is not commonly known. It would have to be a concept that the business plan reader would probably not know; these include machine parts, items only commonly known in other parts of the world, terms that exceed common knowledge, acronyms, etc. However, it can be insulting to the reader if common terms like, supply chain, demographics, management, and financial statements are described and defined in the business plan as business professionals and instructors know these terms very well. Therefore, it is advisable to be considerate to the reader and not assume either way, but rather conduct some research on the target audience (more on that on page 138). Knowing and understanding the target audience is crucial for business plan success after the presentation thereof.

One of the major mistakes that especially students make in their business plan is that they try to "write a paper". They have done so in many other classes on the business topics that are part of the business plan (marketing, operations, etc.). The "paper format" that comes so natural to many is never to be used in a business plan as the business plan will become one document with the purpose of demonstrating data-driven decision making for the viability of an innovation. When descriptions for something, such as fixed or variable expenses, assets or balance sheet, financial statements are found in a business plan, it reads more like a paper and not a professionally written and concise document. Sometimes it even appears that students are "padding" their papers and try to make them longer by adding long quotes or descriptions. This is not professional business writing.

Business plans that employ tools, for instance graphs and charts that the student creates, or cited data from reliable sources are stronger than other business plans that solely employ written descriptions. This is especially true for complicated processes or professional and specific terminology.

For example, a poorly written business plan might start the marketing section with a few paragraphs describing what marketing is. The assumption that students need to make is that anyone reading a business plan would already know what marketing is and therefore defining marketing is superfluous. Even though not all readers are marketing professionals, they would surely know what marketing is and a definition thereof would be redundant, if not insulting.

The purpose of the business plan then is not to describe the concepts (or write a paper on the concepts), but to describe how applications from research and gained knowledge (in the case of students what they have learned from a variety of classes in their business degree) will be used with their innovation and business. This differentiation and comprehension thereof are crucial in order to write a business plan and not a paper about business concepts.

Creating Advance Organizing Paragraphs

A business plan is an unusual document in that it is cohesive and connected and yet each part of the business plan could stand alone. For example, the marketing and operations plans are each researched and written separately, however, these sections of the business need to be interdependent as the marketing plan depends upon the product or service being offered and the operations plan depends upon the marketing being presented. Each section of the business plan should be complete in itself. Some parts might be mentioned several times in the business plan and some issues and topics may be highlighted more than once in the business plan. For example, the demographics are highlighted in the marketing section and described with rich, thick data and yet the operations section will refer to the demographic as the supply chain is developed for one of these four: time to market, quality, innovation, or cost. It is important to understand that not all of those four can be satisfied at the same time and a decision of priority has to be made. For example, a supply chain can either be designed to get the product to market as quickly as possible, or built for quality, or innovation or cost, but it cannot offer all of those in equal measure and priority. The product or service and the mission and vision determine which of the four options for the supply chain will take precedence. Another example is that the mission and vision statements needs to be referred to in several sections in the business plan. A good business plan will leave no question that the mission and vision are incorporated into every section of the business as the mission and vision are the "guiding light" to all aspects of the advancement of the innovation.

Because the above is true it is essential that advance organizing paragraph is used to connect all of the sections of the business plan to create one fluent plan. An advance organizing is a paragraph with at least three to seven sentences that explain what is coming up in the next section. Sometimes papers seem jumpy or a sentence or section does not seem to fit in with the rest of the document. The advance organizing paragraph makes papers and the business plan have a much better flow and explains to the reader what is coming up next. Using advance organizing paragraphs is a huge help for the writer as well, as the writer knows that the topic is going to be divided into three sections and that each section should be roughly the same size (unless by design one of the sections is larger, which would be explained in the advance organizing paragraph). There should be an advance organizing paragraph at the beginning of each of the twelve sections of the business plan.

For example, the advance organizing for the marketing section with a graph of a business plan idea might read (remember, this must not be copied and pasted into a business plan as that would be an Academic Integrity violation):

"The following marketing section is based upon research from a variety of business, academic sources and detailed statistics from the industry for the innovation. The marketing section will be divided into five sections; each of these sections are equally important. The first section will cover the product, the second section will explain the price, the third section will explain the people, the fourth section will describe the place (location), and the last section will detail the promotion strategy."

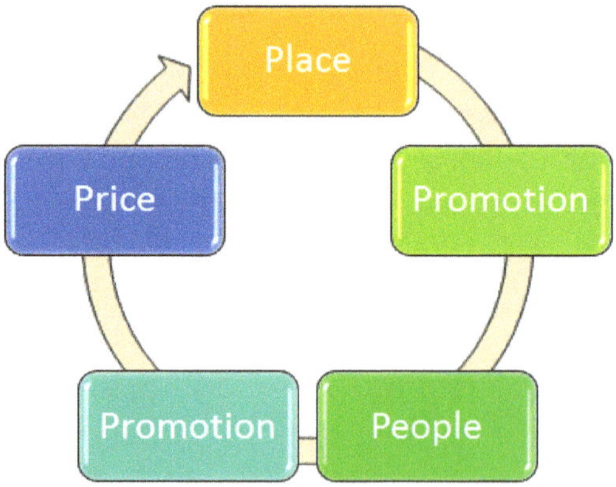

The adjoined graph was developed by Dr. Eckmann using SmartArt to highlight the five Ps of Marketing. A similar SmartArt could be developed in the marketing section of the business plan (highly recommended). Each of the five Ps would be included in the marketing section of a business plan and would be described underneath, as well as introduced in the paragraph above and its use explained in the paragraph below.

If there are more questions and more help is needed on how to write advance organizing paragraphs, the following information should be helpful. Advance organizing paragraphs are a hallmark of business plans. Students, as they move to graduate school, will find this practice is part of graduate school writing as well. Here is a good article on how to write advance organizing paragraphs: http://www.aje.com/en/author-resources/articles/when-its-best-be-explicit-using-advance-organizers-structure-your.

Creating "After-Organizing" Paragraphs

At the end of each of the twelve sections (or more depending upon the innovation) of the business plan there will be a "wrap up" paragraph where the entirety of that section of the business plan will be summed up. An after-organizing paragraph is also three to seven sentences long. Before writing the after-organizing paragraph look over the section and consider all of the Level 2 and Level 3 headings as something from each of those heading should be included in the conclusion, which the after-organizing paragraph is. It is from these headings that conclusions need to be drawn.

It is imperative to remember that the after-organizing paragraphs (like any conclusion) may never ever present new information or ideas as the purpose is to just recap a section. However, the after-organizing paragraphs can be used to segway into the section that is following. An example of an after-organizing paragraph is shown below, taken from Kerstin Young's business plan written during her MBA Capstone class (again, this must not be copied and pasted as the intellectual property belongs to Kerstin Young):

> "All that being said, going public is not necessarily the best way to go and formerly successful companies have been forced back into the private sector to recover after decline in business has hit them and they were no longer able to sustain their place in the public arena. McSherry (2013) shows such an example in his article. In consideration of that aspect it might be advisable for DeducH_2O to abstain from going public and concentrate on private funding and support from organizations pushing green and sustainable businesses. Besides, only companies that are well established and have different options of applying alternative strategies and can face multifaceted obstacles at the same time are advised to enter the public trading arena (Solomon, 2013) and for now, DeducH_2O is not at that stage and will not be for at least past the four-year hurdle."

Creating Visual Displays & Understanding their Importance

Graphs and visual displays should be included at least every three to four pages within the business plan (many very successful business plans have over thirty graphs and visual displays). Graphs and visual displays include maps, financial data, SmartArt, etc. A great example of how to use a visual display would be with the description of the need for the innovation. Visual aids are more convincing and explanatory than wordy descriptions.

Remember, sixty-five percent of all people on the planet are primarily visual learners. See this Forbes article for the reasoning: http://www.forbes.com/sites/tjmccue/2013/01/08/what-is-an-infographic-and-ways-to-make-it-go-viral/#1ddecd3f353c. This means that most people find that visuals are easier and better to comprehend than words and written explanations. For business plan authors this establishes the opportunity to not only create interest with visuals, but also to create understanding of particular difficult aspects of the business plan and the innovation.

Another fact that speaks in favor of visual aids in a business plan is that ninety percent of information is received visually. In other words, people are very used to visual aids and therefore rely and even depend on them. More information on visual intelligence can be found here: http://visualteachingalliance.com/.

For the use of visuals, it is important to apply them correctly. When inserting pictures, graphs, data, etc. remember the following must be included in accordance with the APA guidelines.

1. They have to be cited even if the student created them
2. Introduce them in the paragraph above
3. Explain underneath how the data from the graph will be used
4. All visuals should display similar colors throughout the whole business plan (this creates a "color brand")

Here are the links to said guidelines on how to properly cite them: https://owl.english.purdue.edu/owl/resource/560/19/ & https://owl.english.purdue.edu/owl/resource/560/20/.

Utilizing a Writing Partner & Understanding their Value

In business over eighty percent of all work and projects are completed in teams of two or more. In academia collaborators are often referred to as "writing partners". In business there are a variety of terms used to describe collaboration, including teams, work-groups, squads, companies, pods, and even murder boards. As people move further up in organizations there will be increasing requirements to work successfully in teams. Individuals who only want to work by themselves have relegated themselves to the lowest positions in business as they are known to "not play well with others". The business world relies heavily on business relationships as no company, no leader, and no employee can exist in island status. Collaborations are necessary to keep all aspect prosperous and viable.

Entrepreneurs who are using this book to write a business plan are encouraged to designate a writing partner or two. This person should be chosen wisely as part of a clear picture of who the audience will be for the business plan. For example, if the business plan is written and funding will be required from a mother-in-law the writing partner choices should be completely different than if the plan was being written for funding from a financial institution. More information on knowing the audience can be found on page 138.

For capstone students, success will depend upon their willingness to participate and invest as a writing partner. Writing partner teams are tasked with sharing all papers in a timely manner, leaving time for feedback and implementation of such, before submitting it to the instructor. Students and entrepreneurs who engage with their writing partner will find the following benefits that can make the difference between success and failure (in the respective business environment):

1. The student-to-student perspective gives great insights
2. It gives students someone to brainstorm with who is familiar with the subject material and the class goals
3. The writing partner should catch some of the mistakes in the papers and thus students can improve the papers before the instructor grades the work
4. Students who engage in writing partner exercises tend to get one letter grade higher on every paper
5. Business major students do understand requirements and modalities of the capstone class and the business plan and can remind each other of the details
6. Peer review business skills will be developed that students can use for the rest of their business careers
7. Teamwork and collaboration are critical in business and students will be able to state categorically to employers that they are experienced in working in teams
8. Points are usually awarded at the end of the class for meaningful participation with writing partners; failure to participate with the writing partner then results in loss of points which can move an A-paper into the B range (or from funding to non-funding)

Please note: Each business plan is unique. This is why writing partners should not become overly concerned if their partner's sections are a lot shorter or longer or have fewer or more sources, as each business plan will have a different focus. However, students need to meet the minimum page and minimum source requirements. Students are paired with other students not for comparison or competition, but for brain storming and idea generation, as well as checking business writing compliance (APA, etc.).

CHAPTER V - Mission & Vision

Researching Global Ethics

The following information will assist as Section 2 of the business plan is written. One other thing to remember about ethics is that not all countries have the same standards and laws around intellectual property rights as the United States. This falls back on their leadership and their values. After all, countries are made up of people, led by people who were elected by people, and all of them have their own values and ethical standards. Consider the American Presidential race of 2016. The two major party candidates running for President in that election held vastly different views on almost everything, but certainly on ethics, morals, and rights.

Likewise, many companies abroad and in the US hold very different values. To think that companies have good and solid ethical values solely because they are US based is naïve and shortsighted. Some US companies have gained public attention for their patent trolling. This is when organizations do not offer a service or product, but solely hold and own patents, patiently waiting for another company to produce or offer a product or service that infringes on a patent they own. Then they sue for millions of dollars and that way finance their "business" and pay their employees who specialize in checking for patent infringement. And patent troll firms can be found all over the world. For more information on the topic see the following link: https://hbr.org/2014/07/the-evidence-is-in-patent-trolls-do-hurt-innovation.

Pricing is another great concern when it comes to ethical business behavior or the lack thereof. Just recently, in 2015, Martin Shkrely came under fire when he purchased rights on the AIDS drug Daraprim and jacked up the price by over five-thousand percent than to what it used to be (http://www.nytimes.com/2015/09/21/business/a-huge-overnight-increase-in-a-drugs-price-raises-protests.html?_r=0). Many pharmaceutical patent holders create similar issues, as seen in the EpiPen price battle: http://www.npr.org/sections/health-shots/2016/08/29/491797051/maker-of-epipen-to-sell-generic-version-for-half-the-price.

In reality, companies in the US are commonly less known for issues with patents. For the innovation consider the vulnerability if manufacturing is moved to another country (especially a third world country). For example, Cisco and other manufacturers have their phone designs patented, but once they move manufacturing outside of the US they are not secure that their same phone design will not show up "down the street" with a different name for half of the price. Patent laws are only relevant and enforceable in the country in which they are filed. So if a patent is filed in the United States it does not mean that this patent cannot be "stolen" or infringed on in another country and there it may not be considered theft. Business owners and entrepreneurs need to be very cautious and considerate when it comes to manufacturing products outside of the US and have to contemplate this for their business. Develop a strategy around ethics and patents for the product or service. Look at this short article on how Apple got into trouble recently with patent rights and also look out for patent trolls: http://money.cnn.com/2016/02/04/technology/apple-patent-lawsuit-virnetx.

Connecting Corporate Mission/Vision, History, Performance, Customer Analysis, Industry, & Employees

Connecting mission and vision, history, and performance to the innovation and the industry is strategic and critical work. This is important on three levels because the business plan must:

1. Connect the innovation to the industry
2. Connect the innovation to the potential funding source
3. Connect the company's vision and mission to all

To build the mission and vision the following must be researched, analyzed, and included in the business plan. Remember each of these are going to be covered in different sections of the business plan and with more research the value will become clearer:

- **History** of the industry of the innovation: What are the "new" innovations, what is downward trending? What has success looked like in the past? What are the roots of innovation in the industry? The data collected for this would help to build the mission and vision but also would be part of Section 4, "Industry Trends and Analysis".
- **Performance** is about the trends (financial, culture, etc.): This is research into the history of their stock price and what their culture is like. For example, considering Microsoft and Google, they have very different cultures. Read this short article on Microsoft from

the Business Insider: http://www.businessinsider.com/getting-recruited-by-microsoft-2010-4.

- **Typical customers** are about who the demographic currently in the innovation space is and more importantly what new customer base could be added to it: What is the language that would appeal to the desired customer base? For example, if the customer base is currently millennials and the desired customer base is Gen Y, these two different market segments use language very differently. And the mission and vision of the company will have to appeal to the targeted customer base. Consider the following article from the New York Times (always a great source): http://www.nytimes.com/2016/10/28/learning/lesson-plans/minding-the-generation-gap-investigating-media-portrayals-of-millennials-and-gen-z.html?_r=0. This research would be used to develop the mission and vision and would also be included in the marketing section.
- **Industry** to consider for the innovation (probably will be more than one): Research the trends in that industry and learn about it; reflect what stage of the life cycle the industry is in; study any major lawsuits in the industry; contemplate shortages or changing demographics. For example, what if a student was writing a business plan for a new product for an insurance company? The new product would serve an aging population. The trends in the industry that might be important are:
- What percentage of insurance companies fail to deliver on policies?
- Are the projections for an aging population showing that they are living longer?
- What process does an insurance company have to go through to get a rate increase?
- Who is the "big dog" in the industry right now? What is their profit margin?

This would be helpful to know to develop the mission and vision and would also be included as data for Chapter 4.

- **Employees**: There is a good article from Fortune Magazine (2004) on the recruiters at Google that might also be helpful: http://fortune.com/2012/02/24/inside-googles-recruiting-machine/.

So, Microsoft is interested in fit, but they appear to have very high standards and one mistake and you are "out". While Google appears to be recruiting a lot of people and has the highest rate for recruiter to number of employees, what hints do these short articles give students about the culture of these organizations? What hints are provided to create a meaningful and culturally relevant mission and vision? See what articles can be found about their recruiting practices, as recruiting practices often give an excellent glimpse into a company's culture. Find out if there are any pending lawsuits and if those lawsuits have a common theme (check out Wal-Mart on lawsuits) and see this article: http://www.washingtontimes.com/news/2014/dec/31/suing-wal-mart-bad-business-practices-lead-litigat/. Information learned in this search could be used to help build the management section.

- **Mission and vision** statement development is the foundation of the business plan: Like the SWOT analysis during the writing of the business plan, the mission and vision will be refined and improved as research continues. Remember the SWOT analysis is developed in Section 4 and then refined in Section 5 of the business plan.

CHAPTER VI - Strategy Defined in the Context of a Business Plan

This portion will assist in the writing of Section 4 of the business plan. The purpose of this text is for students and entrepreneurs to demonstrate and apply everything they have learned in their business studies, both inside and outside of the classroom. Completing a business plan will provide an overview or strategic view of how businesses work. The business plan format will help to show the progress in their learning and the ability to communicate with decision makers in organizations about the breadth, depth, and the entire scope of a business idea. Students of business who create successful careers are able to understand the restrictions and opportunities of each function of a business (from innovation, through operations, marketing, finance, etc.).

Many who are undereducated or unprofessional only view organizational structures from the point at which they are competent. An example would be a person who works in marketing and thinks that everything in an organization revolves around marketing decisions and discounts or chooses to ignore the important influences of finance, operations, industry trends, and the needs of management. But the successful student of business is able to see the entire scope of an organization, regardless of where they are working, what they specialize in, or what they are passionate about. Similarly, someone who works in the operations department may initially be unaware of the constraints that marketing faces. Some remain unaware of how limitations impact available but commonly limited resources. However, after completing this business plan, the author will be able to view their organization or organizations in general from the wide angle, so that they will become aware of various challenges and opportunities. Therefore, the business plan will give access and a full understanding of the entire opportunities and interdependencies of business mechanisms. As each section of the business plan is developed, a deeper understanding of the complexity of business and how each part of a business must work in concert with the other parts. This broad view of business is how competencies are created.

It is a good policy to have more than one arrow in the quiver of innovations. This means that it is best to have three to five ideas and/or variations of the initial idea for an innovation. For example, if the entrepreneur's innovation is "boots that can make you fly" then it would be advisable to consider different variations. These variations could include "pants that make you run fast so it feels like you are flying" or it may turn out that it takes "a shoe and sock combination to make you fly". The lesson here is to be sure that the initial idea for the innovation is flexible enough to be influenced by research, cost, time to market, existing and changing target markets, practicability, and financial viability. It is important not to take the criticism and what the research indicates personal as it is key to remember that a business plan is built to meet the needs of a market segment, not the needs of the business plan writer. This goes back to the knowledge that opinion ("I want this company because I want the product, no matter if others do too.") bears no weight if data does not support it ("There is no market demand for the product."). This is a lesson that is often taught in the Spike TV show "Bar Rescue" where bar owners frequently created the type of bar they wanted to hang out in, not the type of bar the market in that area supported, hence they needed their bar "rescued".

As research develops and continues it will become clear which of the innovations or variations thereof are the best choice. It is also advisable not to "fall in love with" one part of the innovation over another as it can create bias in the research and its outcome. An innovation that does not provide enough research material or that has an unfavorable research outcome should not be chosen for the business plan (again, the decision needs to be data-driven, not opinion-based). Some will still proceed with an unfavorable idea and find out too late into the development of the business plan that the innovation is not feasible. That way they might end up having to retake the capstone class or redo the entire business plan, which will put it far out of the timeline. During the development of the financial section, which will be dealt with during the last third of development, money or control issues with the innovation will become obvious. Unfortunately, at this point it is too late to rewrite the papers with a different innovation. A rough estimate on the financial viability of the business idea early in the process is therefore advisable.

Note: If the business plan writer has either professional or personal experience (maybe as an employee, volunteer, or even as a consumer) in an industry, that could be a perfect place to look for innovations. For example, if someone works on old cars on the weekends as a hobby and can think of a lever or a tool that is not available at this time but would assist all of the "weekend garage mechanics", then that could be a great place to look for an innovation. Alternatively, if a student is a new parent and serious consumer of baby products, the former experiences (both positive and negative) within this field could prove to be excellent field work for an innovation. Ideas and creativity can be born out of any need or desire for improvement and/or perfecting. Remember, it is always best to start a business plan with these three words: "There is a need."

Understanding the Need for Strategy

The first reason for an increased need for strategy is that there have been irrefutable major shifts in the economy and in how business works today. In the earlier years of the American economy, before the 1970ies, markets were more stable and defined. For example, there was less competition and companies were known for manufacturing one product or offering one service. IBM is a perfect example. They first developed mainframe computers during the Cold War, then they manufactured PCs; in 2005 they stopped making PCs and in 2014 they stopped making servers. The following article offers insight on this matter: http://www.wired.com/2015/01/z13-mainframe/. Companies morph into perceived value for customer demographics projections more quickly than ever before. For each of these major changes, innovations and shifts in what a company offers, a new or adjusted business plan is needed.

The second reason, more patents for new products and services were filed in 2015 than any of the years before, as seen in the following government statistics report: http://www.uspto.gov/web/offices/ac/ido/oeip/taf/h_counts.htm. This means that more people have ideas they would like to turn into businesses. Coming up with ideas is wonderful and necessary, however, sculpting the ideas into a business plan is like having a marble block and chiseling away the hard rock to expose the sculpture that is the business plan. The business plan is thc fruit of labor after the seed of the innovation is planted.

Once students decide on a business plan idea, the innovation, they must have it approved by their instructor. Then the research begins and it is critical to think about the business plan from the perspective of the two analyses below. Think about what is known or knowable and what is unknown. Apply dancefloor - balcony thinking to the innovation and consider what and who the needed elements are. Reflect on the business plan in another way as well; think about the adaptive and the technical challenges that the particular business plan will face; create the roof, then build everything underneath; and then address the challenges step by step.

Strategy is a realistic and workable plan to accomplish a change or an innovation. Existing business plans are often reworked every time there is a change in management or a change in direction for an individual or an organization. Strategy, just like keeping a house clean, requires constant vigilance and additional resources and often a complete rethinking of the structure and contents. Strategy is subject to change based upon external changes and events and internal resources, for example an adjustment in the availability of funds and a host of other internal and external variables. Strategy is a scientific, research-based, and analytical look at what currently is and what could be in the future. A business plan is the road map from what-is to what-can-be. Strategy is necessary when a change or improvement has been identified and the desire is to "bring to life" the change or improvement.

Successful businesses run on well thought out strategy; unsuccessful businesses often "wing" it and will misidentify opportunities and waste precious resources (time and money). Without a thoughtful and researched strategy, organizations underestimate the potential value, scope, demand, and cost of an opportunity. Organizations that do not have a strategy are often disrespectful to their employees, stakeholders, and stockholders that have invested their time, talent, and energy into an endeavor. Thus, strategy is a research-based, conscious, and thoughtful approach for action to complete a specific and desired outcome. With strategy comes the recognition of an opportunity and the research-based data-driven decision making to demonstrate step by step how the opportunity will create value. Most people can think of someone who has a great idea because they can identify a shortcoming and envision a solution, but these types of ideas do not come to success because there is no implementing strategy.

"Strategy may be one of the most overused and misused terms in society today. Everyone has a "strategy" for virtually every activity in their lives. These range from those what might truly contain legitimate elements of a strategic decision to those that are completely inaccurate uses of the term" (Bamford, 2008). For example, many people do not have and do not need to have a strategy to "run" their homes. A successful business, in contrast, that is running a rehab center with twenty plus clients has to have a strategy. Thus, that successful rehab center would research elements that increase the success rate of sobriety for their clients. This would include food that increases clarity of decision making, the acquisition of that food, researched behaviors that lead to sobriety, and actions steps that help clients and the rehab center to incorporate ways of behaving that will lead to sobriety. So every action of every employee, stakeholder, and client is thought out and researched in advance and adjusted to complete the goal of helping each individual client to become and remain sober.

Strategy is the child of management and business. Management has been studied for centuries, including ancient authorities like Plato, Aristotle, and Machiavelli who were interested in the ways that an end game could be reached with the fewest of resources. Great links for more information on these intelligent men can be found here: http://www.leadershipclassics.org/assets/boa.pdf & https://mbsportal.bl.uk/taster/subjareas/busmanhist/mgmtthinkers/machiavelli.aspx.

One of the more recent gurus in business is Peter Drucker. Drucker's ideas have stood the test of time and are as relevant in 1942 when he entered the realms of GM as a business specialist, as they are today. Peter Drucker is often referred to as the "Father of Business". His ideas have changed the way that business runs. He brought a fresh, pragmatic, and thoughtful approach to making a business successful. Read more about Peter Drucker at: http://www.druckerinstitute.com/.

It is often recommended that a heading be "Drucker's 5 Questions". Drucker, Hesselbein, and Kuhl (2015) developed five essential questions that are at the heart of management. These questions need to be asked early and often as an organization grows. It is surprising how many key players in companies cannot answer these five questions. For the management section of the business plan consider answering each of the following questions:

1. What is our mission?
2. Who is our customer?
3. What does the customer value?
4. What are our results?
5. What is our plan?

It is not surprising that key employees of many failed businesses were unable to answer these questions. As the business plan is prepared, stop and think about the answers to these questions. It is very wise to add a section to the business plan where these questions are asked and answered to give everyone who reads the business plan a clear understanding of what is important to the business. After all, the innovation and business need to reflect the writer's intent.

There is a famous Drucker quote, "culture will eat strategy for breakfast" (this quote is also attributed to a number of others including Steve Jobs), that refers to the fact that culture must be aligned with strategy in order to reach success. Culture is described as the ways that people think, act, and work within an environment. For example, if the pay systems for an organization do not promote innovation (for example, three percent raises for everyone regardless of contribution) and if there is little to no recognition for those who innovate, then having a strategy and a business plan that calls for innovation will most likely fail. Strategy needs to align with culture and culture needs to align with strategy. This means that the business plan must provide a step-by-step, research-based, and careful explanation of how the culture and the strategy will work together for success within the context of the industry, location, and the business. This needs to be supported by research within the industry, location, and the demographics of those who will work within the business. The ways that individuals will be attracted, developed, and retained in a business will be a large influence on the culture development (for good or for bad). This is not only a cost factor (after all, high turnover rates are a huge expense and financial burden on businesses), but can also greatly affect how a company is viewed by potential customers.

For the business plan the different cultures that will be a part of the new business need to be addressed. These groups include, but are not limited to, the product, the industry, and those who will build, sell, and buy the product. The business plan will have to promote communication and authenticity among all of those people and cultures. This is an example of a potential clash in cultures that would need to be addressed: Assume that the business plan is going to offer a simple product to a demographic of high income customers. Those who will build, market, and sell the product are most likely not going to be the consumers or the target market of the product. This resulting clash in cultures would be clearly identified, researched, and data-driven solutions need to be offered in a successful business plan. Please note that makers do not have to be users, but the gap will still have to be addressed, explored, and explained. Full disclosure of positive and negative aspects within the business is crucial for the sake of the credibility of the company.

For example, at a five-star hotel the front desk personnel are probably not going to make enough money to be able to stay at a hotel of this class, cost, and quality and may not have spent much time with people who are well-off. This means that the hotel staff will need training and education on how to interact with high income and wealthy hotel guests and how to attend to their needs, wants, and demands. There is a wide variety of people that work at a five -star hotel, as the stakeholders include the cleaning staff, the wait staff, the spa personnel, cashiers, bankers, etc, and there are the customers as well. However, with attention to the culture of the five-star hotel, with all of its wide variety of personnel, they can be connected through a mission and vision that creates a culture of trust, patience, and customer-centric attitude and that mission will connect all of this diverse amalgam of personalities and stations of life.

So how should strategy meet culture? Strategy requires both, research on all contingencies and goals for action within the culture. The goals for strategy need to be the generator for action. A successful strategy will include research and action for incorporating the completion of the outcome that is desired through the strategy on ways to inculcate the strategy into an existing system (culture). For example, when Hewlett Packard decided to spin off the Apple brand they had some of the Hewlett Packard employees show up to the Apple facility as new employees for that endeavor. Most of these HP employees came dressed in their usual business attire, suit and tie. At the Apple facility the orientation phase included the cutting-in-half-the-ties of those who were newly joining the Apple team. This small symbol of "cutting the cord" with the parent company created an emotional, visual, and memorable example of a culture shift from HP to the Apple endeavor (Personal communication, John Couch, 2008). This type of clarity can create loyalty as workers feel connected to the product and the company. Thus Section 5, "Strategic Positioning" and Section 9, "Marketing, Management, and Operations" of the business plan need to be closely correlated.

Creating Strategic Intent

Strategic intent will be included in Section 5 of the business plan. It is a way of thinking that creates short-term goals connected to a larger picture.

It is sometimes similar to the mission or vision statement, but often deeper than that. Strategic intent is the "one thing" that will be done right and first, every time possible. Strategic intent is evidenced by the fact that each employee, no matter where in the organization, is aware of the "one thing" that needs to be done every day in every job. In this scenario employees are aware where the company is heading and understand their commitment and what they bring to the company to achieve that goal. The greatest challenge for strategic intend is for the workforce to grasp that all created positions are important and necessary for the achievement of the professional goals.

With strategic intent the big picture has to be crystal clear to every stakeholder and every stakeholder has to have a view of what they will individually "win" by participating (Eckmann, 2012). Major corporations and startups often use strategic intent to be sure that all employees know exactly what to do when. Another reason for creating and disseminating a strategic intent is to give employees the option to make decisions without checking in with management every time. For example, Southwest Airlines, the 44-year-old airline is known for its friendly (and often witty) flight attendants, as well as its top-notch customer service. This stems from its employees-first mantra, which plays out in a trickle-down effect. In order of importance, Southwest ranks employees first, customers second, and shareholders third. "We believe that if we treat our employees right, they will treat our customers right, and in turn that results in increased business and profits that make everyone happy", the airline explains in a blog post about its company culture. The full article on Southwest Airlines can be found here: http://www.businessinsider.com/southwest-airlines-puts-employees-first-2015-7.

If employees feel disconected to the strategic intent they will often be disengaged and less productive. When staff holds a different, higher or lower, standard than the employer there will be a loss in productivity. It is important to consider while writing a business plan what the strategic intent of the business is, what will the "guiding light" be, etc. Doctors have the Hippocratic Oath, "do no harm", so that doctors, insurance companies, and all of those in the medical field should have their "guiding light", their strategic intent be "do no harm". For more information about the Hippocratic Oath read here: http://www.pbs.org/wgbh/nova/body/hippocratic-oath-today.html.

The strategic intent needs to be evident in all parts of the business plan and be connected throughout especially the mission and vision. It has to be a thread that is clearly the code by which business will be conducted for all personnel at all times. For example, if the strategic intent is to "listen to the customers and meet their needs", then in the marketing section of the business plan and the operations plan would incorporate a call center and methods for soliciting customer feedback and listening and changing processes to meet customer needs. The operations department would be especially aware of the needs of the customer in the design, development, packaging, transportation, and recycling of the product or service. Additionally, the action plan would include concrete and clear ways that the customer feedback and implementation thereof will be a customary way of conducting business. This would be consistent throughout the entire organization. It also means that the business plan can be opened at any point and the strategic intent will be clear, concise, and consistent.

Utilizing Strategic/Critical Thinking

This section, like Chapter 2, can be counterintuitive and often brings about a whole new level of thought. Chapter 2 focused on becoming more of a creative thinker. This section will provide an in-depth and yet practical analysis of how to sharpen thinking skills. So please be patient with the process. What is strategic or critical thinking? There are probably one hundred ways to answer this question as businesses and academics like to debate this topic. Instead of engaging too deeply into the discussion, two positive and practical examples will be provided on how to improve strategic and critical thinking. The first is Dancefloor-Balcony and the second is Adaptive-Technical (Heifetz, 2009). (Picture source: http://blog.readytomanage.com/wp-content/uploads/2012/09/critical-thinking-comic.jpg)

Heifetz (2009) describes the dancefloor-balcony strategy essentially as a helpful tool to imagine that a small group of observers goes to a dance long after it has started. The band is playing and people are dancing. Further imagine that the observers move to a second story to gain a "bird's view" of all that is going on at the dance (the band, the dancers, the non-dancers, the gaps between dancers, non-dancers, and the band). The following is a personal example of that application by Dr. Eckmann as it occurred in September of 2013.

Recently I noticed that I got angry in a meeting. I had just offered a new idea during the meeting and no one seemed to pick up on my idea. I thought the idea was pretty good. So at first I was surprised and disappointed that no one seemed interested in it. About twenty minutes later one of my co-workers (let us call him Bob) brought up exactly the same idea I had introduced only twenty minutes earlier. I thought surely someone would comment that the idea had already been proposed by me and that I had said the same thing. But to my utter amazement no one did. It was as if Bob's idea was brand new and unheard of. So I got angry and started an internal dialogue about how I am often misunderstood and other negative comments (all self-focused dancefloor matters).

However, after a few moments of internal self-loathing I was able to change my perspective and go to the balcony to look at this situation from the broader view, from the viewpoint of the others: At first, when I looked around the room I noticed that I was sitting by myself at one end of the table while everyone else was rather crowded down at the opposite end, closer to Bob. I also noticed there were six people in the room, three women and three men and that all of the women were sitting closer to me than to Bob. Next I thought about the subject matter, which was really more in Bob's area of expertise than mine. I knew Bob had been with the organization far longer than I and was a hard-working and well-respected employee. About four months earlier, Bob was given another job and I took over his previous position. I remembered that I had felt some competition from him ever since then. From time-to-time I sensed Bob was playing one up with me. But I also knew that he had been a help to me at different times.

What the balcony perspective allowed me to do was to focus on the others in the group, especially Bob, and not only myself. Instead of looking at the situation solely from the dancefloor and feeling sorry for myself, or angry, or frustrated, I needed to strategize what might have been going on throughout the entire group, not just myself.

The dancefloor view would not solve the problem, nor do much to increase my effectiveness in the group. But the balcony perspective allowed me to start looking for the "unseen forces", the motivators, backgrounds, and other factors that exist all along and which need to be seriously and strategically considered before, during, and after making an intervention into a group.

Interestingly, what I needed to consider in this situation, among other things, was a bit of humility. I was relatively new at this position and likely had not yet earned the respect of my co-workers. I probably still looked like the "new kid on the block". I could easily have come off like someone who was trying to make a big first impression or even show off. Maybe I was smug or unkind or even insensitive to Bob's recent change of position; maybe Bob was unkind as well, but I needed to take a strategic look at my own part of the dynamic. If I sensed he was being competitive, was I likewise? Who started it and did that even matter? Who was continuing the potential power struggle? And to what overall purpose? The organizations? Or individual agendas?

Self-application Strategies: Imagine that someone viewed the above experience of Dr. Eckmann, as many have probably experienced something very similar. Using what has been learned, review this or a personal situation, analyzing it from the balcony and the dancefloor view. Now take a moment to answer the following questions:

1. What would observers see from the balcony view that they could not see from the dancefloor?
2. What details and perspectives would be clearer from the balcony view rather than the dancefloor?
3. What strategic interventions could have been made that might have been more successful (hint: anything is more successful than self-pity)?

Remember, it is much easier to work on ourselves than others and to work on our own situation rather than on developing the strategies of analysis of the "whole" situation. And even more importantly, to make somebody else look bad does not make ourselves look better (personal communication Young, 2016). It is important to remember that just by making someone else "shorter" we do not gain height. Including more data in the decisions in life is always helpful and the dancefloor-balcony view is a very productive way to look at professional and personal experiences.

Different views produce different data. Data-driven decision making is increased by changing perspective. Strategic analysis includes being mindful of the broad view, the narrow view, and gathering data from both. With more data the interventions become more powerful, effective, efficient, and more often than not only then possible.

Creating Strategic Plans

This portion will assist in the writing of Section 4 of the business plan. Strategy becomes indispensable at the intersection of an identified opportunity and a desire to create additional value. This means that when a person, group, team, or organization identifies an opportunity and desire to bring that opportunity to life, research is needed to create a step-by-step strategy to bring that opportunity to fruition. When success is not guaranteed, and it never really is, when an opportunity is desired, strategy is the bridge between opportunity recognition and value creation.

Strategy can be used both, personal and professional. An example of personal strategy is that many people live strategic and organized lives. They manage their time and their resources in an efficient way to maximize their lives. For example, some people have a strategic intent to be sure that when they are older they have enough money to live a comfortable life. These people are more likely to live with fewer short-term pleasures (like a $4.00 coffee each day at Starbucks, which adds up to almost $1,500 a year), so that in the later years of their lives they can travel or help their children financially. It is a great idea to look at all of the habits and determine if they are worth the expense when viewed from the "balcony of our lives".

In this context it is important to add information to explain how to develop a stronger strategy for personal finance. It is crucial to understand the "Rule of 72" here, which is a calculation that shows how much money can grow when it is invested early in life. The calculation considers the future value of money, a concept that is taught in the finance classes in the MBA program of all schools. The following link explains the "Rule of 72": http://www.investopedia.com/ask/answers/04/040104.asp.

So if someone were to save $1,500 a year from age twenty to sixty (forty years), that would be worth approximately $130,000 at retirement age (depending upon rate of return). The "Rule of 72" explains the exponential growth of money over time. In fact, Einstein said "Compound interest calculation is man's greatest invention" or "compound interest is the greatest wonder in the world". Here is a calculator that does exactly that calculation and can be used to determine the worth of saving money early: http://keisan.casio.com/exec/system/1234231998. This interesting article is on the investing habits over a lifetime, known as the Life Cycle Hypothesis: http://www.investopedia.com/terms/l/life-cycle-hypothesis.asp.

Another example is that many people live a strategic life with their health. They do not smoke or drink to excess and they exercise; they may eat more vegetables and less processed foods and they may spend four or five times a week exercising rather than sitting in front of a computer playing video games. When someone has a strategic intent concerning their lives, they think about what their long-term plans are (in any area) and they take small short-term steps necessary to reach those goals. People who are not strategic say things like, "it will all work out" and sometimes it does and sometimes it does not, but generally speaking long-term success professionally or personally takes some thought and short-term sacrifices to meet that long-term goal. Strategy means setting small short-term goals to reach the big long-term goals.

The best game to practice strategic thinking is chess, the epitome of strategy. Chess requires thought and vision as to the consequences of actions. Children as young as twelve years old have become grandmasters of chess, as this article shows: https://en.chessbase.com/post/game-changer-at-four--youngest-che-player-250613. What does that say about strategy? It is a state of mind, a state of thinking, and even a state of life. It is an ability that can be learned and applied at any age, to any life challenge, personally, professionally, or leisurely.

The enemy of strategic thinking is typically habits. Habits can be either good or bad, but many habits often are unexamined and continue without good reason. In contrast, strategic thinking requires a mindful examination of behaviors and a knowledge of the fact that everything we do has consequences. Exercising (usually a good habit) was probably started with a thoughtful value of health. Smoking (usually a bad habit) is often continued without thoughtful examination of the long-term consequences. The reasoning for habits can be examined with knowledge and thought.

What we value drives what we think; our thoughts drive our decisions, and our decisions drive behavior. Thinking deeply about what we value and to notice when there is a continuation of a habit that is not working or leading to a more productive life, requires an examination of the values that are held highest. To use the Starbucks example again, if every day another Starbucks' coffee is bought, even though the intention was to make their own (infinitely cheaper) coffee at home, then an examination of values is in order. Here are a few strategic questions to consider:

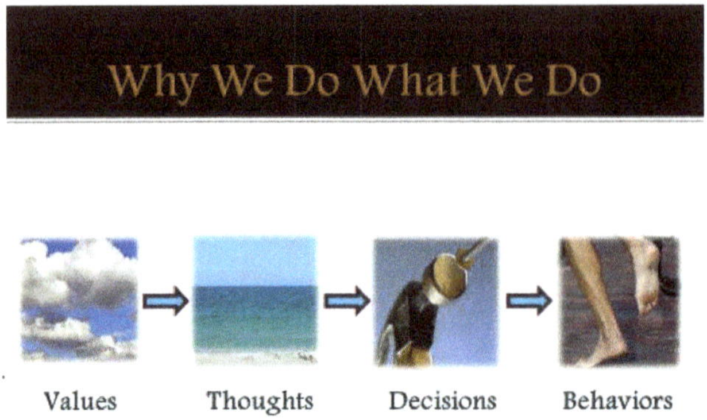

1. Could a thorough examination of the disconnect between what I want and what I do create a strategy for change?
2. How would I spend my time and money differently if changing took no effort?
3. Which of my values need to change (hint: "I should get all I want now, no matter what" is usually not a great value) to achieve my principles?

Personal change and strategic thinking often are a precursor for developing and implementing an innovation. Many successful business people first changed themselves in order to create a successful business. We practice personally what we incorporate professionally. An example is the idea behind the development of the nicotine patch as a short term strategy that could create change. Another illustration includes the story of Michaela DePrince who set her mind as a young unloved girl at an orphanage in Sierra Leone to become a famous ballerina and so she did through dedication and hard work. Read her story here: http://www.amightygirl.com/ballerina-dreams.

The list goes on with Elizabeth Warren, the hardworking Senator from New York, who had to start working at age nine, babysitting for a family across the street, waged as a waitress at twelve years old, and became a Harvard Law Professor in her twenties. This woman clearly knows the value of hard work, dedication, and the will to develop a successful career. For more about Elizabeth Warren can be found on her website: http://elizabethwarren.com/elizabeth.

In short, strategy is needed for anything that people want to accomplish that is intended to bring a positive change or greatly increase value. Strategy is the vision and the action plan to make something worthwhile happen. Remember, strategy is the alignment of both, balcony and dancefloor view. "Balcony" is the large bold vision for a major long-term value driven goal, while "dancefloor" are the exact steps needed to accomplish that goal (Heifetz, 1994). To learn more about the concept of dancefloor-balcony please review this explanation: http://practical-step-by-step-solutions.blogspot.com/2010/06/looking-down-from-balcony-to-lead-on.html.

The following section will continue with the topic of strategic thinking, offering the concept of adaptive and technical strategic analyses as they were briefly introduced in above segments.

CHAPTER VII – Analytics & Financials of the Business Plan

Preparing a Preliminary SWOT Analysis

This part will apply to Sections 4 and 9 in the business plan. One of the analyses that is expected in a business plan is the SWOT analysis (and it is common practice to call it just SWOT), for the innovation and the Fortune 500 company, if applicable. **SWOT** stands for **S**trengths, **W**eaknesses, **O**pportunities, and **T**hreats. While strengths and weaknesses are internal aspects to every part of the organization, opportunity and threats are external to the organization. External influences are harder to steer and change than internal ones and therefore demand even higher thoroughness in evaluation.

Data for the SWOT analysis comes from the business plan research. It will begin with the literature review and will continue throughout the entire writing of the business plan. The SWOT analysis is a profound starting place for research as it names the area for said research and will give key insights into what is known and what is unknown, as the business plan is initiated. It is really a questionnaire that assists in the formation of operational functions of the business. A SWOT analysis is never actually complete or final. It can always be extended as new information is uncovered. It should be done early in the business plan development. Like with all other parts of the business plan, especially as it is done in stages through the process of writing the business plan, updating the SWOT analysis up until the final business plan is presented, as more information for the SWOT analysis is revealed, is crucial.

So, the SWOT analysis never ends. SWOT analyses should be the driving force for the vision and mission statements. If business plan writers can find a SWOT analysis on one or two Fortune 500 companies that are within the industry would be excellent data to use to determine the Fortune 500 companies' interest in the innovation, and with that create an indicator that the business plan might be accepted by an investor. The Fortune 500 company may not call this type of analysis SWOT, but it is easy to review their data and to extrapolate this information from financial statements and other researched material. For the thoroughness of the business plan the recommendation is to perform a "preliminary SWOT analysis" and then after more research and analyses are prepared a more data driven "main SWOT analysis" (see page 95) is performed.

This kind of breakdown is helpful when adjustments are desired by a company at a future time. The SWOT analysis is used as the business landscape for changes. For example, if the costs of goods begin to increase exponentially, then a SWOT analysis would be used to consider alternatives. If the product or service is more of a success than the data originally indicated, then the business leadership would review the SWOT analysis to consider the alternatives for increasing value and success.

The form below from www.SCORE.org is an excellent starting place. Also note that Score.org is an excellent source for a great array of topics and issues within the business plan. Business plan writers have contacted Score offices that are near to their home and met with representatives (for free) to get excellent advice. They have also contacted them in the desired location for the innovation for additional information. Discretion and the amount of help that Score associates (note, most people "working" there are actually volunteers and do not make any money) can lend is determined by the local office. Score is manned by local volunteers so they may or may not have time to help business plan writers that develop a project for school. But many business plan writers attribute some of their success to the help from Score. Business developers (entrepreneurs) may have priority over students at Score, but it never hurts to ask.

SWOT Analysis Worksheet

Fill out the fields below and review with a mentor. This information can help you outline goals and strategies for your business and marketing efforts.

	Strengths	Weaknesses	Opportunities	Threats
Product/ Service Offering				
Brand/ Marketing				
Staff/ HR				
Finance				
Operations/ Management				
Market				

Can any of your strengths help with improving your weaknesses or combating your threats? If so, please describe how below.

Based on the information above, what are your immediate goals/next steps?

Based on the information above, what are your long-term goals/next steps?

Analyzing the Industry & Trends

This segment will assist in the writing of Section 3 of the business plan, "Industry and Trends Analysis". Industry for the purpose of this text will be defined as a larger group of similar businesses that are profitable or create value. The industry is the general field in which the innovation will arise. This is the economic, social, and general information on the industry. For example, as an entrepreneur is writing a business plan on designing a new "never go flat" tire for race cars, then the industry would be the automotive industry. The business plan should have a minimum of five to seven pages of industry analysis which would consist of five to twenty business and academic sources. Another example, if the innovation is to create a new pump to give medicine to patients in the hospital, then the industry would be medical. Remember, in the business plan to apply the analysis not to describe it. An application gives the business plan developer an excellent opportunity to demonstrate all that they have learned. As a reminder, an analysis often includes phrases like, "this demographic analysis will be applied in the following four ways to create success. . .". If there is a need for more details on industries, the following link is a good choice to follow as it drills into each industry category: https://www.osha.gov/pls/imis/sic_manual.html. Below is a brief and incomplete list of industries:

Agriculture	Construction	Financial
Retail/Wholesale	Transportation	Information
Financial	Professional Services	Education
Health care/social assistance	Leisure/Hospitality	Federal/State/Local Government
Self Employed	Manufacturing	Utilities

Learn more about these industries and find a detailed list at: http://www.bls.gov/emp/ep_table_201.htm.

It is important to note that most products and services fall into multiple industries. For example, a new water meter would fall into manufacturing as well perhaps federal state and local government or retail and wholesale, depending upon the business plan goals and the customer base that is being targeted.

The trends are the general direction (growth, financial, market share, etc.) of the industry. Commonly four to ten years of trends are researched and analyzed (a trend can only be established with research and citations). For example, is the industry showing upward trends, generally attracting more customers, is it more profitable, more popular, or is there a downward trend attracting fewer customers, less profitable, or less popular? But this is not always the case, analysis will paint a clearer picture of the trends.

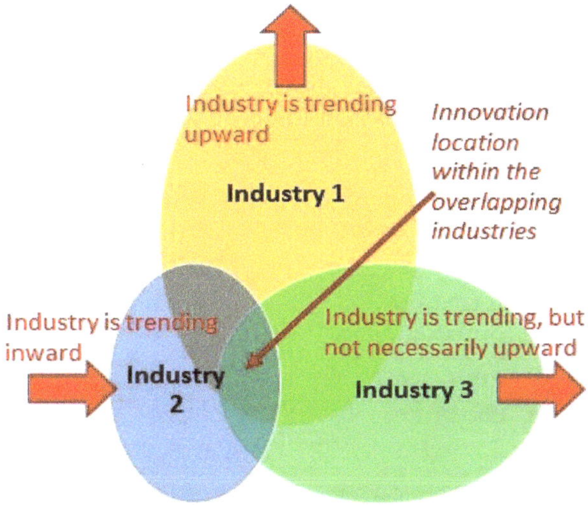

It is best to find at least one of the industries that is part of the innovation and trending upward; this might not always be the case, however. In other words, it might be safer for the business to find an industry with positive trends. Then again, some very successful business plans were designed to save a dying industry or maybe just create a process (service or product) improvement that will attract new customers, create financial value, and therefore "save" the industry.

This type of graph could be used in a business plan to create a visual display of the industry. Also remember that it is never enough to just have a graph; all graphs and charts need to be explained with words and describe relevancy. Words and a picture are always the best plan. Please keep in mind, this graph cannot be copied and pasted into a business plan. This is because, one, it would be plagiarism and two, all graphs and visuals have to be tailored to the business plan they appear in, to picture a description.

In this context, please review course materials or visit the Blue Ocean Strategies link: https://www.blueoceanstrategy.com/. The concept of "blue ocean" is that an industry that has "room" for development and change is better than a crowded industry or "red ocean". For example, smart phones are found in a very crowded industry and the barriers to entry, as well as the competition, could be overwhelming. A "blue ocean" is an untapped and un- or underdeveloped market where there is a proven need for a new product or service. Great and new ideas often create the "blue ocean" where no one has thought to bring a new product or service to fruition. To quote Star Trek "go where no man has gone before". For "blue ocean" ideas it is critical that as soon as possible a patent or a copyright is applied for, as others will be trying to crowd in as soon as the product or service reaches the marketplace.

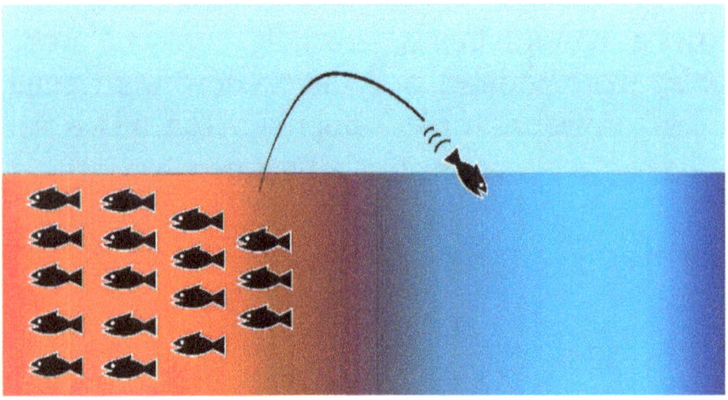

Business plans are usually most successful when the writer can demonstrate that the innovation will thrive in, or better yet create, a "blue ocean" scenario. Interestingly the mission statement of "blue ocean" companies is integral to their business. This is a great time for business plan developers to think about how their business plan (from marketing to action steps) will be built around the mission and vision and also how the trends will work within the chosen industry. More information and the picture above can be found on the following sites: http://www.tbsreg.com/wp-content/uploads/2016/07/red-ocean-blue-ocean-1.jpg.

Knowing the Competition

This section will assist with the writing of Section 5 of the business plan. Research, starting with a literature review, will give a clearer picture of the competition. Competition may come from within the industry or from the outside. It is important that the competition is evaluated (using APA research) from all possible angles. Research can determine and uncover the most likely competitors. Some find using this website helpful: https://biz.yahoo.com/p/sum_conameu.html, but also remember to think, who else could become a competitor in the future? Therefore, it is important to consider the past, present, and future competition. As with all profound data, there can always something be learned from it.

The types of players within an industry are changing with technology. Recall the example given on IBM on page 89? Another example is that not too long ago the only competitor that Barnes & Noble Booksellers had to concern themselves with was Borders and a host of local "mom and pop" businesses that sold books. Now the competition for Barnes & Noble is Costco, Wal-Mart, and especially Amazon. Not too many years ago Barnes & Noble evidently did not imagine that people might prefer to read an electronic book rather than a paper book (one of the authors likes to read paper books while the other prefers eReaders). Even though Barnes & Nobel is holding steady (see this article on the issue: http://www.forbes.com/sites/marcgerstein/2016/06/01/quo-vadis-barnes-noble/#6fcefd9c509e) only time will tell whether they can overcome their current and potentially future competitions.

So, for the innovation think deeply about future competitors and include that in the business plan. Also think about others who might enter the marketplace and compete for market share for the innovation. Barnes & Noble leadership were probably surprised to see "Big Box" Costco as a competitor. As the innovation is developed it is important to think which parts of the innovation will become "core competencies" and which parts of the innovation could eventually be outsourced. This consideration has to be evaluated from the view point of competition. This is because any additional service or product features can possibly attract more competitors. For example, it could happen that the product in itself would operate in a "blue ocean", but the service that is offered with it could lie within the "red ocean"; as a result, the entire innovation would attract more competitors than potentially necessary and outsourcing the service could prevent just that.

It is also good to provide a visual display of the potential competition. This means that a chart (often using SmartArt) on the competition for ease of viewing of the relationship would make sense. Here is a great supportive YouTube video on how to create and develop SmartArt charts and designs, if business plan developers are not familiar with that Microsoft Office tool: https://www.youtube.com/watch?v=IKDgkQG-9zI. Some business plans have very elegant and intricate graphs, charts, and pictures (this can be achieved using different tools and even SmartArt). The creator, however, must ensure that the visuals are not too complicated to be understood by the reader, the audience. Often overly complicated graphs can lose the elegance and can get confusing. This would make the visual application counter-productive as it is meant to help explain the concept and not confuse the reader. The sophistication of a visual aid should not outweigh its informative value.

Determining Locations & Demographics

This will apply to multiple sections in the business plan, specifically, Section 2 and 7, "Mission, Vision & Innovation Description", and "Marketing", respectively. Successful business plans begin with an innovative idea and then immediately drill down into the data surrounding the location and the demographics. The location usually drives the demographics. Location is a broad category as it can include the location of the manufacturing, the location of the customer base; the location of the call center for an online business, etc.; overseas or domestic. Tax considerations, funding; patents; or a potential market for future sales are all driven by demographics.

For example, if the innovation is tailored to create more management jobs for veterans in manufacturing, then the research would focus on locations and would show the number of veterans who have the right education and are ready for promotion. Please see the information below on Fresno, CA that might be a good location for employing veterans. Read the data and see how that might work. The best demographic data (and often location data) is almost always found in .gov sources.

- Locations:

  The following chart is an example of .gov data on the City of Fresno, CA. Research for an innovation in Fresno is a significant factor. This data could be embedded directly into a business plan (with proper citations). It would show information on Fresno as a customer base, manufacturing location, or distribution center, depending upon the business plan.

http://www.census.gov/quickfacts/table/PST045215/06019

Population	
Population estimates, July 1, 2015, (V2015)	974,861
Population estimates base, April 1, 2010, (V2015)	930,452
Population, percent change - April 1, 2010 (estimates base) to July 1, 2015, (V2015)	4.8%
Population, Census, April 1, 2010	930,450
Age and Sex	
Persons under 5 years, percent, July 1, 2015, (V2015)	8.2%
Persons under 5 years, percent, April 1, 2010	8.5%
Persons under 18 years, percent, July 1, 2015, (V2015)	28.7%
Persons under 18 years, percent, April 1, 2010	29.8%
Persons 65 years and over, percent, July 1, 2015, (V2015)	11.5%
Persons 65 years and over, percent, April 1, 2010	10.0%
Female persons, percent, July 1, 2015, (V2015)	50.1%
Female persons, percent, April 1, 2010	50.0%

As an example, if a business plan was going to be targeting veterans (either as employees or as customers) in Fresno, CA, then this information would be critical to be included:

Population Characteristics	
Veterans, 2010-2014	42,072
Foreign born persons, percent, 2010-2014	21.7%

http://www.census.gov/quickfacts/table/PST045215/06019

Education	
High school graduate or higher, percent of persons age 25 years+, 2010-2014	73.2%
Bachelor's degree or higher, percent of persons age 25 years+, 2010-2014	19.5%

http://www.census.gov/quickfacts/table/PST045215/06019

So, take a moment and take this self-quiz after going to the link to get the data:

1. What is the percentage of veterans in Fresno?
2. What percentage of adult population has a BA degree in Fresno?
3. What percentage of the population in Fresno recently changed?

4. Trick question: What percentage of the businesses in Fresno are manufacturing?

Now think about the answers to these questions and how they might create data for making a case that Fresno is an excellent location for getting veterans manufacturing jobs.

Location is a critical part of the business plan and supporting the choice of a location must be supported by data, as all decision making is. The US Census data is always considered one of the best sources for location and demographics. But beware, one data set from the U.S. Census is not sufficient to make a case for a business plan. Other data will be needed and will have to be researched to determine answers to the many other questions, including these:

1. Does the population of Fresno have enough housing?
2. Are there other cities that have more veterans?
3. Are there other cities that have more manufacturing?
4. Does the demographic have a future?
5. What other industries are successful in Fresno?

The data above on Fresno is an example of exactly what needs to be done in every business plan. It is important to ask the questions in the business plan of who, what, where, when, and how, which is most often covered in demographic research. Every business plan needs to have these details discussed and covered. Even negative data needs to be shown. While it is true that it can make a case against a decision, it is still crucial to address it. It would need to be done in a way that reflects the awareness of the threat for the business, but also why the pro-decision was still made and how the risk will be overcome or faced. This type of honesty is crucial in a business plan because it is better to deal with the "devil you know" rather than be surprised later in the product or service development. In addition, the business plan writer should not hide or neglect certain possible shortcomings as it is dishonest and shows short-sidedness.

Opinions are interesting, but they are not data. Opinions can start the business plan, but that is not where a business plan is created. Sometimes business plan writers think that just because it would be "wonderful" for them to have this innovation come to fruition in their current location, it is an executable idea. That opinion, however, needs to be demonstrated using data-driven decision making. After research it may become apparent that the business plan writer's location is not the ideal location, but another city or even a city in another state my offer more success. Choosing the wrong location can cause the failure of the business plan and also the failure of the innovation as a whole.

- Demographics

Typical demographics factors include age, gender, marital status, race, level of education, income level, occupation/employment, and as aforementioned, location; but also factors, such as, religion, birth rate, death rate, average size of a family, average age at marriage, and home ownership are considered demographic data.

Business plans are always about data driven decision making. Yet, everybody is part of demographics. So if the innovation would be

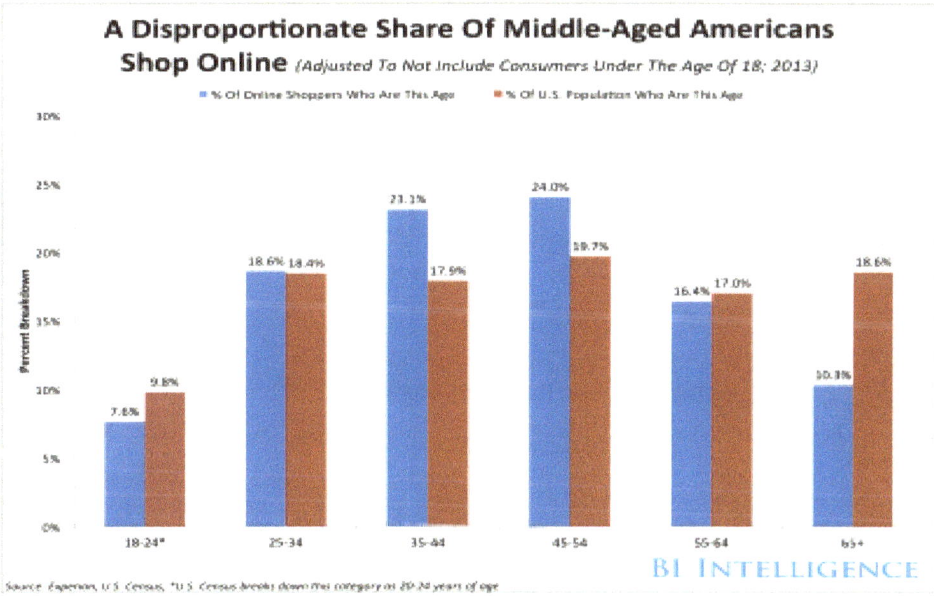

something that the business plan writer and his or her friends would purchase, then they need to begin researching data that would substantiate that claim. For example, the following graph from the U.S. Census might be used to support a claim about how the demographic shops online, http://www.businessinsider.com/the-age-demographics-of-who-shops-online-and-on-mobile-2015-4:
A successful business plan has a clear picture (supported by data) of the demographics of the customer, potential "ready to hire" employees, trends, and how the customers will purchase the product

or service (online, in-store, etc.). The age, preferences, and financial situation of the customer is known and supported by solid data. These are usually graph accompanied with paragraphs of explanations. The above chart featuring online shopping creates multiple data points for a business plan, these include, but are not limited to:

- Channels for distribution
- Ages of potential customers
- Marketing place
- Packaging and materials
- Cost of materials
- Accounting
- Billing

Please note, embedding these types of charts as shown above, directly into the business plan is an excellent idea. The general rule of thumb is that each section of the business plan would have two to five graphs or charts (cited in APA). Each chart must be relevant to the particular business plan and section it is presented in. However, before importing and using any data, ask and answer these questions:

1. Is there a citation for this data? If so, is it referenced in APA and listed in the reference section?
2. Is the graph applied rather than just explained?
3. Is the graph or chart introduced (so it does not seem to fall into the paper without warning)?
4. After the graph, is the data carefully explained in the context of the innovation?

If any of these questions are answered with "no", the material needs to be revisited, revised, and/or completed before the information can be used in the business plan.

Mining Data & Trends

Fortune 500 companies provide many positive examples for business plan development. However, just because a company has a positive financial statement it does mean that the company will provide a positive role model for ethics, sustainability, or treatment of employees (for example, check out the history of Wal-Mart). All data from Fortune 500 companies needs to be carefully evaluated. So, use information from the Fortune 500 company to benchmark several select sections of an innovation as the basis for the business plan.

Trends create demands in that an upward trend or "trending" people will start buying trending products and services. For example, when MTV started being successful, a market place opened up for the clothing, the jewelry, and other fashion items shown there. Also, with Facebook a market trend for advertising, even target advertising opened for opportunity. A third example is how the cell phone market opened up the opportunity or trend for "apps".

Entrepreneurs need to show evidence of viability through research, focusing on the demand for the innovation. This is called trends. The goal is to substantiate that there is a need for this innovation based upon industry research. The trend is often found in the financials of Fortune 500 companies; it could be suppliers, customer demographics, and even distribution outlets. Trends are somewhat unpredictable and forecasts are more often wrong than right. However, data from trends can be one indicator for the creation that suggests demand and shows where an opportunity exists.

Trends can also show that opportunities are declining and that it is not a good time to enter a market with a new innovation. Sometimes a trend will indicate market saturation. Trend lengths may vary based upon industry; technology has a pretty short shelf-life (some indications show three years). A trend can also reverse. For example, head phones had become smaller and smaller over time and the one fitting just in the inside of an ear were all the rage. Then with Dr. Jay creating a trend, the "the bigger, the better" of headphones was created. Consider the history of cellular/mobile phones (see https://www.washingtonpost.com/news/the-switch/wp/2014/09/09/the-history-of-the-mobile-phone/).

There too, "the smaller, the better" has become a trend. Now (2016) Motorola is selling cell phone attachments that, even though adding features like a projector, a camera with zoom, and speaker, make the phones bulky again (see https://www.motorola.com/us/moto-mods).

Research that is data-driven can show that the innovation is clean, clear, and not too complicated (no legal restrictions, supply or manpower shortages, sustainability concerns with no contract HLE minerals). Oliver Wendell Holmes (Supreme Court Justice) stated, "I would not give a fig for the simplicity of this side of complexity, but I would give my life for the simplicity on the other side of complexity" (2006).

Remember the two feet of innovation from page 25? The right foot innovation is a brand new idea and the left is a major process improvement that creates a new demographic or revenue stream. A left foot innovation is not just a logical extension of what is already coming next. It is often identified with the idea that someone would abandon the current product or service and pay more for the new process improved innovation. A rule of thumb is that the process improvement would create ten to fifty percent more market share in the same industry or another industry. For example, going from a standard white board marker to a neon colored white board marker is not a major process improvement as most people are not going to throw away the standard marker for a neon one. However, when Mr. Sketch created "scented markers" that was a process improvement or a left foot innovation, as the appeal for the new type of marker created a whole new revenue stream with value.

The business plan could be for either "foot" of innovation, or even both. However, it is important to note that innovation can be "created" or it can be found through trends. An example of a created innovation (right foot) are advances through technology that shaped the platform for the creation of an affordable and transportable cell/mobile phone. How many knew or saw the need for a cell phone until they were available? How many people knew that they needed a cell phone watch until those become available? Anyone can be a visionary and come up with these ideas, but it takes practicing the skills mentioned before (like Mind Maps, Time-Outs, and dedicated times for creative thought combined with the value that data-driven decision making demonstrates) to make an idea a successful innovation in form of a product or service. The opposite of a created innovation (or right foot) is one that follows trends or is a logical extension of something that is already available (left foot of innovation). This could have been a lighter, much thinner cell phone, or one that also had email and internet connections, when they first came out in the late 1990ies.

Against common perception, it is not easier or harder to develop a brand-new innovation (right foot) or a major process improvement (left foot). Consider the innovation, is it a brand new idea? Is it a logical extension of an existing idea? Either way, make it clear and based upon industry trends and data-driven research to make a case that the innovation is unique, critical, necessary, and will create a new revenue stream or add value. Warning: A left foot innovation is NOT an extension of something similar that has already an existence; it must provide a viable and identifiable new market stream. Also remember, "good will" is not a direct revenue stream and will frankly not meet the financial criteria for successfully completing a business plan. Instead, if a new innovation is being invented, the information that explains the right foot innovation will need to be even clearer as the reader will have less context for what is being offered. This is while with a left foot innovation the reader may be able to have a personal experience or a shared vision with the industry or the product or service, as the reader may have used an earlier rendition of the innovation.

Developing the Main SWOT Analysis

This information will be used to prepare the main SWOT analysis in Section 5 of the business plan. A preliminary SWOT analysis was prepared earlier (see page 103) and now it is time to dig down and refine it. The SWOT analysis is one of the places that funding sources will view carefully. Funding sources are going to want to know that the writer of a business plan has carefully and thoroughly researched and reported on all of the strengths, weaknesses, opportunities, and threats of the innovation.

This is a step-by-step process for including the SWOT analysis in the business plan:

Write about seven to ten sentences that explain the SWOT analysis below. Then create a visual representation (students can create this by going to a Word document and creating "SmartArt").

After the graph, it is recommended to have subheadings for strengths, weaknesses, opportunity, and threats where there is detailed and APA cited information for each area. The SWOT analysis usually takes four to five pages to detail and needs to be cited. Each section of the SWOT analysis would contain relevant data and sources on location, industry, trends, and the connection between the Fortune 500 company (if applicable) and the innovation. For example, if the Fortune 500 company has had a downward trend in innovation or even sales, the innovation could provide for them a new revenue stream. In addition, if the Fortune 500 company has done a lot of research in the field of the writer's innovation then that would provide a strength for thereof. Another example is if the Fortune 500 company has a core value and strength in marketing, the power, scope, training, and reach of the marketing department at the Fortune 500 company could provide a strength for the innovation. So to be clear, the SWOT analysis is not ON a Fortune 500 company but some of the strengths and opportunities could come from Fortune 500 companies.

The top five or six findings should be evident in the literature review. The SWOT analysis is going to highlight the key and critical components of the innovation. This will be displayed both, graphically and then explained in detail. Note that the graphics for the SmartArt should be of complementary colors for all of the other graphics in the business plan. For example, a business plan for an ocean front restaurant might have all "ocean blue" graphs, while a business plan for a new tool to be used to change tires might be all in black and white.

If there are more questions on SWOT analysis and SmartArt, view the following sources:

- Learn more about the SWOT analysis: http://www.mindtools.com/pages/article/newTMC_05.htm, http://ctb.ku.edu/en/table-of-contents/assessment/assessing-community-needs-and-resources/swot-analysis/main; this is from the Score.org website, which means it is a valuable source: https://www.score.org/blog/your-first-step-toward-business-growth-swot-analysis
- Learn more about SmartArt: https://support.office.com/en-us/article/Create-a-SmartArt-graphic-fac94c93-500b-4a0a-97af-124040594842?ui=en-US&rs=en-US&ad=US

Formulating the ROI

This segment will apply to Section 9 of the business plan, "Financials". Return on Investment (ROI) is a quantitative measure of the cost versus the returns for a particular investment or innovation. Money must be spent and invested and the exact amount of money that is gained from that investment must be clearly shown. ROI is also used to compare one business opportunity to another (see "opportunity cost" on page 124). ROI is an analysis or calculation that helps to determine the viability of an option or opportunity. Anyone providing initial funding for a business plan will want to see a strong section on ROI. The following slides were prepared by Dr. Eckmann and her students for the Operations class in Brandman University's MBA program:

What is ROI?

1. ROI is net profit divided by the cost of investment times 100 to get a percentage
2. There must be a "cost of investment" and it can't be just a cost savings. You have to invest money on the front end.
3. For example, students pay for tuition to get an MBA. They also invest time. Those two are quantifiable. So students invest time and money into their education and the additional money they will make when they graduate would show a ROI.

How do you demonstrate ROI?

1. ROI = Net Profit / Cost of Investment * 100 = %
2. There **must** be a "cost of investment" and it can't be just a cost savings. You have to invest money on the front end.
3. Example:
    - Selling lollipops for $1.50. The lollipops cost $0.50 each (investment). Net profit from sold lollipop is $1.00.
        - ROI = 1.00 / 0.5 * 100
        - ROI = 200%
    - In this scenario, you received a 200% return on your initial investment for the lollipops.

In application this means, as a business plan writer analyzes the ROI for buying an electric car and it would cost $5,000 more than the same car that is non-electric, the next step in the ROI section is to measure and analyze if the cost of the electric car would provide a good return on investment. The calculations for it would look something like this:

Electric Car	**Non-Electric Car**
Initial cost: $X	Initial cost: $X
MPG of the vehicle: X mil/gal Multiplied by the cost of gas per year (based upon the cost of gas and the average amount of miles that you drive a year)	MPG of the vehicle: X mil/gal Multiplied by the cost of gas per year (based upon the cost of gas and the average amount of miles that you drive each year).
Rebates available? HOV-Lane Accessibility?	Environmental costs?
Maintenance expenses? (anything extra to consider about the electric vehicle?)	Maintenance expenses?
Probable resale value - based upon Blue Book or "Car Facts"	Projected resale value - based upon Blue Book or "Car Facts"

After these financial computations are completed, stop and think about any other considerations that are important that could impact this decision. The ROI is always backed up with data and "good will" might be a line item (like "environmental costs" above), but these types of esoteric considerations are never the major factor for determining ROI. A note about environmental costs: There are ways to be able to save money and be more sustainable at the same time. Sustainability can have an ROI. For example, manufacturing a product that uses less water is better for the environment, but most often good for ROI, or reducing the amount of plastic that goes into a bottle means that it will be cheaper to manufacture, ship, and recycle. So there are real environmental savings that bring financial value. However, remember that using sustainability as a public relations endeavor does not always result in financial value; so keep in mind, ROI is always about financial value and viability first. Please keep in mind, there can be no ROI without a financial investment. For additional information on calculating ROI and other financial computations review this website: https://financial-calculators.com/roi-calculator.

CHAPTER VIII - Strategy, Structure, & Risk

Performing an Industry Analysis

This section will assist in the development of Section 3, "Industry Analysis". The industry analysis is an important part of the business plan. This is the foundation for building what is being brought to the marketplace. This section usually has a graph or a chart of the competition. Some business plan writers perform a second SWOT analysis in this section, which is encouraged. This is an example of some sources that could be used: https://www.sba.gov/blogs/conducting-market-research-here-are-5-official-sources-free-data-can-help.

An example of a competitive analysis on the industry for a new line of plus-size clothing for Macy's could look like this:

Name of competitor	Website	Explanation of why they are a competitor	Volume of sales in plus size clothing / trend
Amazon			
American Apparel			
Banana Republic			
Express			
Forever 21			
Gap			
H & M			
Nordstrom			
J C Penney			
T.J. Maxx			
Wal-Mart			

Analyzing Risk Factors

This section will assist in the development of "Financials", Section 9 of the business plan. Risk is a fascinating concept and requires deep thought, research, and analysis. Risk is often very real and yet often subtle. Risk can be an exposure to something dangerous and it can also be about gaining or losing something that is highly valued. Risk is playing with the fantasy argument of "what if?" and then asking all of the macro and micro questions that could affect the outcome of the success of the innovation and the business.

Different organizations and industries value dissimilar objectives. For example, the criticism of education is that educational institutions (K-12 and up) value protecting administrators and teachers more than giving students an education; a disparagement is that fast food seems to value "fast" more than "food"; a condemnation of technology is that they value "new" more than sustainability. Consider the industry that the innovation resides in, what the values are, and what the inherent values and risks portrait. Economic risk is often analyzed using the "Six Steps of Economic Decision" from Samuelson and Marks (2015). The six steps are:

Step 1: Define the Problem
Step 2: Determine the Objective
Step 3: Explore the Alternatives
Step 4: Predict the Consequences
Step 5: Predict the Consequences
Step 6: Performing a Sensitivity Analysis

The sensitivity analysis, also referred to as "what if?" or simulation analysis, is a way to predict the outcome of a decision given a certain range of variables. By creating a given set of variables, the analyst can determine how changes in one variable impact the overall outcome and the other variables. For more information, visit the Investopedia website here: http://www.investopedia.com/terms/s/sensitivityanalysis.asp?lgl=no-infinite.

Remember that just like a personal budget, organizations have limited amounts of resources. If an organization decides to implement an innovation, it is at the cost of another option (opportunity cost). Organizations often do not have the financial means or the bandwidth to implement too many innovations at once; so choices always have to be made and justified, short- and long-term. More information on opportunity cost can be found in this three-minute video: https://www.google.com/?gws_rd=ssl#q=opportunity+cost.

https://blogs.lawrence.edu/economics/2011/10/dilbert-and-the-opportunity-cost-of-time.html

Consider this scenario: An organization has saved one million dollars to install low flow toilets into its seventeen offices which are located in a drought area of Southern California. The ROI (return on investment) on the low-flow toilets results in expense savings from the water bills that will amount to 1.5 million dollars in five years. These are conservative numbers as the cost savings are depending on the cost of water today and the projection is that the cost of water is going to increase exponentially in the next few years. This same organization has been presented with a different innovation that addresses the issue (perhaps a student's business plan). If the organization implements the innovation they cannot also implement the low flow toilets. The ROI on the low-flow toilets is easy to calculate and to prove. The innovation? That might be a different story. Students have to ask themselves, "what would I do as CEO?"

Deliberate the risks for the innovation with the following questions (remember there could be hundreds more).

1. What is the risk of not pursuing the innovation?
2. What if the competition implements this innovation as well or instead?
3. What other opportunities are being turned down to make this innovation work?

4. What is the risk in being first to market (does the second to market usually make more or the most money)?
5. What is the risk that someone else has already come up with this idea and they are further along in production?
6. What is the risk of having laws or standards change?
7. What is the likelihood of persecution?
8. What is the risk that the consumer will not value the innovation?
9. What is the risk that another innovation will make the first proposed innovation worthless?
10. What is the risk of economic downturn that will dry up capital for funding?
11. What is the risk that the macroeconomic market will change and the result is the target market has to move the innovation from "needed" to "wanted"?
12. Will one political party create more opportunities for the innovation? (It is not always what people think.)
13. Have some of the risks (financial, culture, morale, etc.) to the organization, if the innovation fails, been considered?
14. Have controls to manage both, inside and outside the organization for either massive failure or massive success been implemented?
15. Are there sufficient controls developed and established that will monitor the controls and when?

To answer the above questions means considering all angles of opportunity cost and as it becomes obvious, it is a tedious but necessary process.

Creating Strategic Positioning

This segment will assist in the development of Section 4 of the business plan. The goal of strategic positioning is to create a competitive advantage. Competitive advantage is a deep and interesting topic and is the study and implementation of creating strategies that lead to medium to long-term profitability and value. For example, it is important to begin by thinking on a macroeconomic level about these strategic positioning questions:

1. Why are firms in diverse or similar industries different (for example, Apple, Dell, or Samsung) and seem to attract very different cultures and/or customers? What are the differences between those cultures and those customers? What caused those differences? What is appealing to one customer but may not be appealing to another. But how was this difference determined and how was it dissimilated to the customers?

Some people would never buy Apple products, some people would only buy Apple products (none of their competitors'). Where and how did Apple create their strategic positioning?

2. What makes a business successful over time? In other words, looking at trends in particular industries, why do some types of products have a very long run of success and why do others become "one hit wonders"?
3. It is up to the business plan to make a case that the industry of the innovation will be attractive in the long-run. These factors (used to be referred to as "rules of thumb") are often referred to as Key Success Factors (KSFs) or Key Performance Indicators (KPIs). These are:
   a. **Structure**: What is the current structure of the industry? These give the "rules" for an industry. The fast food industry structure is pretty obvious, "more fast than quality food". Fast food restaurants are open long hours a day (some 24 hours) and tend to hire minimum wage workers and have a high turnover rate.
   b. **Conduct**: What is the current conduct of the industry? Is the industry highly competitive? Made in America? For more information on the importance of American Made read this short article from Consumer Reports (the ads to join cam be ignored): http://www.consumerreports.org/cro/magazine/2013/02/made-in-america/index.htm
   c. **Performance**: This usually refers to the financial performance over time or trends of performance, which are available in the financial statements of the major contributors to an industry, especially if they are Fortune 500 companies.

Consider the questions above and think from the balcony level about the industry of the innovation. Study what the research indicates about the KSFs and KPIs like structure, conduct, and performance for that industry. The resulting data should be included in the business plan.

Depending upon the innovation, the internet will help with the research. Remember, financial data is always available (to varying degrees) for Fortune 500 companies. Some of the websites will not give access unless the user has a subscription, always check to see if there is a thirty-day trial available, and barring that access can usually be gained through brick and mortar or libraries. There is often information from the New York Times, Bloomberg, and Forbes which can be accessed through school libraries, but can require subscription when accessed otherwise. Strategic positioning is found through research. This means that placing the right product at the right time in front of the right customers. Once again, it is important to think of ourselves as a target market.

For example, would someone who used to go to Macy's or Nordstrom to buy make-up go to a beauty supply store to buy shampoo and conditioner. Both of these products are now available for purchase through Amazon Prime. So if some demographics are getting goods into their homes using a different method, then perhaps others in that "demographic" are doing the same. So notice the changes in the spending habits of friends, neighbors, and relatives as they are a demographic.

In the business plan it is never acceptable to write anything like "I like it so others will like it too" (as that is opinion). But it is excellent work to write something more like this; "Through research on hands of friends, neighbors, and relatives it was discovered that purchasing habits were changing and buying using Amazon Prime was becoming more frequent. With that in mind, research began to determine whether this observation was part of a demographic shift or whether these purchasing habits were an anomaly. The triggered research revealed that . . ..". Then start citing and making the point of this dramatic shift using business and academic sources.

So, to create strategic positioning there is usually a triangulation of the data. This means that business plan writers need to substantiate the choice of a position from three different separate research streams. For example, if the innovation was to develop a product and the choice of marketing distribution is through Amazon, then the following three streams of research would be pertinent:

1. What is the history, process, cost, risk, etc. of using Amazon as a distribution system (probably four sources)?
2. What is the particular need that the particular product is being developed for filling (probably five sources including .gov data)?
3. Who is going to buy this product? Do they have the cash to purchase, is the product replacing something else they are already purchasing, why would the demographic switch to the new product (lower cost, higher reliability, easier to use, more attractive, etc.)?
4. Is the use of Amazon cost depending? If yes, how much is too much? If Amazon would drastically increase cost, would customers venture off and buy elsewhere?

Once all of that data has been accumulated and analyzed, then the strategic positioning can be projected. Remember, for different products or services the above questions would differ. If a service is being offered, like an additional offering from Best Buy's Geek Squad, then the case would need to be made that the customers can, will, and want to pay for this new service.

It is not enough to collect all of the data as that is only the first step. Strategic positioning is determined when the research is analyzed and projections are able to be made based upon the accumulation of all three data points (triangulation). Some students ask why "three" and that is a great question, the answer is, because most often it is. Most of the time if a point can be proven with three separate data points from three different data sets (history and trends, need or desire, and/or demographic, for example), then that is considered to be a stronger analysis.

With one source confirming the need from one particular data set is less likely to be valued. If a business plan was to show that young mothers want to buy a better and more collapsible stroller, that alone would not create strategic positioning. But if the data about the need and want for a better more collapsible stroller is combined with the data that shows the demographic has the resources to purchase the new stroller and that it will be a vast improvement over previous strollers, then that creates a very strong strategic position for the use in a business plan.

One last warning, opinions are not going to create strategic positioning, this is proven only through viable academic, sometimes scientific, and business sources. Opinions are based on beliefs, interpretations, and personal points of view, while facts can be proven by research and data. The business plan should therefore only display facts and fact-based predictions and not opinions. If strategic positioning continues to be unclear, the link below is a free online course that is offered through Score.org: https://www.score.org/event/creating-strategic-plan.

CHAPTER IX - Marketing, Management, & Operations

Considering the First & Second Moment of Truth (FMOT & SMOT)

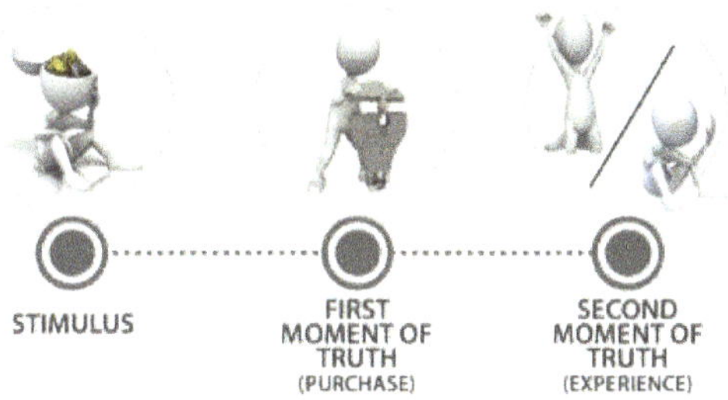

This part will assist in the development of multiple sections of the business plan: sections, 6, 7, and 8. As the business plan is being built it is important to consider the experience of the customer and/or consumer. This information on the experience of the customer is significant from the beginning of the supply chain to the end. The reason why it is crucial is that the materials that are purchased, the assembly of the product or service, and the marketing of the product or service needs to have in mind, at all times, the customer experience. An example is women's clothing. There are some customers who make their purchasing choice due to the materials that are used in the product; some customers will forfeit design for the "feel" and "wearability" of the material used. So to consider the customer experience only in the marketing section of the business plan would be a mistake as the customer experience already begins with the materials used for production.

An example of not considering the ramifications of naming a product and the target demographics was when Chevy named one of their car lines "Nova". The word "nova" means a "brightening star" however in Spanish the words "no va" means "no to". Chevy neglected to research and consider the First Moment of Truth for an entire population demographic by naming the car line "Nova". What was supposed to mean "new" (in Latin "nova" means "new") or "star with increasing brightness" (that is what it means in the field of astronomy) became a perfect example of how the breadth of research needs to include all facets of the innovation and the reaction of potential customers. For the Hispanic community this naming was a flop and "no go". Even large successful Fortune 500 companies sometimes forget to do all of their homework in form of research. With in-depth data-driven analysis from research it is possible to avoid making this type of mistake. There is no upside to turning away a demographic. It is all about customer communication and in that ensuring that the message is not ill perceived.

As the business plan is in the ideation stage it is important to consider the innovation in terms of customer motivation. This means that from the beginning of the development of the research for the plan, motivational theories are employed. According to Psychology Today, the strongest motivation is fear, followed closely by pride (see https://www.psychologytoday.com/blog/the-main-ingredient/200909/the-most-powerful-motivator). However, doubt is a motivation killer. It is important to think about not wanting to have customer reaction to be primal, like fear, as the customer will respond with the "fight or flight" reaction, neither one of which will get them to purchase the innovation. This means that the message needs to be more elegant and the appeal to the customer and the assuage of any feelings of doubt. The goal is to appeal to the customer without having them have any negative or even neutral reaction, but to put the product in their cart or use the service without too much thought. Judgements like "this is nice", "this is easy", or even "this is fun" are the desired responses. This messaging will be on target with research and with a deep understanding of the target market.

Consider the following instance: Car manufactures moving into the van market discovered that the placement and size of cup holders was very important to the female demographic that was more likely to be driving the van (usually with a pack of kids) to and from school and sporting events. However, some mistakes have been made of "over-segmenting" the market demographics. Read this short Harvard Business Review article from 2009 (usually considered outdated, but after evaluation, the information is still well-fitting in today's society) that goes over some of the history of demographics and market segmentation: https://hbr.org/2009/01/why-a-good-cup-holder-is-so-ha.

The following section will describe two ways to consider the customer experience, the **F**irst **M**oment **o**f **T**ruth (**FMOT**) and the **S**econd **M**oment **o**f **T**ruth (**SMOT**). Remember there is no chance to have a second "first moment of truth" or leave a second first-impression. This means that if the customers' first reaction to seeing the product is negative, the chance of success for the innovation is greatly reduced, if not eliminated. It is important at the inception of the innovation business planning that the customer experience is thought through with research and great attention to detail.

FMOT: When the customer first sees the product on the shelf or the service advertised, the following questions are raised AND answered within a split second:

- Are the packaging and look attractive?
- Are the colors that are used going to appeal to the demographic (some colors and/or color combinations have a negative impact on some cultures)? An example is that white roses are used for a funeral in the US and thus would probably not be a good symbol for baby products.
- Does the packaging match customer expectations for the product to be used? An example is that hygiene products more often use blue (safe and clean) rather than red (dangerous and dirty), probably for obvious reasons.
- Does the customer have an emotional response that makes them feel confident that the product will deliver what is promised?
- Are the basic materials used going to be attractive to the customer demographic?
- Is the language on the marketing materials and the packaging going to a broad and yet specific demographic?

SMOT: When the customer first uses the product and the following questions are raised AND answered:

- Does the customer experience the desired results?
- If the product is going to vary greatly from other similar products, is this explained to the customer adequately? For example, when laundry detergents and dish washing soaps are liquid or in smaller packaging on the inside, will the customer be surprised and unhappy, or is the smaller packaging explained (e.g. with the number of loads it will clean or it needs to state "concentrated", etc.)?
- Is the smell, touch, weight, and volume as expected?
- If the product is concentrated does it appear more expensive by weight?
- Does the customer see real differences and results?
- Does the experience of the customer match the expectations found in marketing materials? For example, if the product boasts being

ecofriendly, is there a reduction in the usage of plastic in the packaging? If not, the inconsistency will cause a disconnect for the customer by sending conflicting messages.

There is a need to research and consider the FMOT and SMOT for the product or service that is being offered and work on designing and delivering a positive experience for the customer. This is a critical part of the business plan and the customer experience needs to influence every part of the business plan, from the very beginning to the very end of the supply chain.

Developing a Marketing Plan Analysis

Marketing is a key component of the business plan. Ultimately it does not matter if a great innovation is developed, if the supply chain is seamless, and if the management plan is cutting edge if there are no customers to purchase (and re-purchase) the innovation. Marketing, like all of the other parts of the business plan, is developed using research and analysis that is clear and comes from viable and respected sources. For the marketing section much of the demographics most often comes from .gov websites. For example, this data set could offer multiple reliable sources for an innovation that is housed in or will sell to San Diego citizens: http://www.sandiegocounty.gov/hhsa/programs/phs/documents/CHS-Demographics_NorthCentral.pdf.

Review .gov data early and often as most often data from these sources will be found in several places in the business plan. Remember, it is not professional to use the same data over and over again (for example, the average age of a Latino male in San Diego). But from the above data set there are a variety of segments that could be used to build a marketing plan, for instance:

- Number of people with health insurance by age group
- The languages spoken (good to know for advertising promotions)
- Education levels
- The types of industries that are prevalent in San Diego
- Age distribution

Here is a link from Score on the marketing plan: https://www.score.org/resource/marketing-plan-guide.

Now is a good time to remind the business plan writer to stay with the habit of continuously scanning data for useful information. Not only does this create experience and proficiency, but it also helps to utilize and to assess the full data set and not just the most obvious information. Data that does not appear of value when it is first viewed may turn out later as the business is developed to be critical information. It is a great habit to keep a list of research sources (and how to get back to it) as the business plan is being developed. There are different ways that help with information re-accessibility:

- Save the website in a designated folder under the favorites on the computer
- Print out the document with the source attached to it
- Save the document as a PDF file with the source included
- Create a reference page (in APA) & save it to the computer

It is important to keep in mind that all presented data must be relevant to the section and business plan. Also, the business plan needs to explain the data and walk the reader through why it was chosen, how it is used, and why it is relevant; the context must be obvious. Do not expect the reader to filter through data in order to understand it. Any misinterpretation and confusion must and can be avoided. Data from .gov sites will provide a key source for a location; population distributions become clearer for the innovation with data from .gov that can provide data sets that utilize the five Ps. The following are some examples of how to utilize the five Ps in a variety of innovation business settings.

Example 1: Farm to fresh restaurant

A student might run a restaurant catering to health conscious and highly socially responsible singles and families. To position this restaurant towards the target market, he or she might consider having:

- **Product** - Food catering to those who value sustainable food production and taste. Children's menu that is tasty and also meets the desires of parents
- **Price** - Willing to pay more for local sourced food, smaller portion sizes

- **P**romotion - Advertisements at Farmer's Markets, "healthy grocery stores", "organic" magazines, etc.; connect with any local vegan and/or vegetarian groups
- **P**lace - Location and opening hours suited to somewhat wealthy singles and families
- **P**eople - Staff who are friendly and personally interested in sustainability and able to speak to the value of farm to fresh while being effective and efficient to the needs of singles, parents, and children

Example 2: High-end bicycle shop

A student might run a high-end bicycle enthusiasts' shop. To position this business towards this market, they might consider having:

- **P**roduct – High-end bicycles parts and repairs for outdoor-loving adults who live an active lifestyle; guarantee quality work for the repair shop to minimize risk and create valuable reputation; have a strong name for the business that is attractive to target market and tells the story of what the business offers
- **P**rice - Those who live active lives from age sixteen to sixty, who have high-quality standards and have the financial means to support an expensive hobby
- **P**romotion - A Facebook page to promote the business online; local bicyclists who have won races or of some notoriety for coffee and "carrot muffin nights"; these could be held at the shop or at outdoor venues frequently used by bicyclists
- **P**lace - An in-town location easily accessible by bicyclists with plenty of bicycle parking
- **P**eople - Friendly and knowledgeable staff, who ride bikes or did ride, who like to meet other cyclists; the repairs shop needs to be run by a certified bicycle mechanic who can guarantee the work

After reviewing the examples above, consider the innovation that is being created. Consider the five Ps and how these will be incorporated into the industry, location, and products and services that are to be offered. Each of the five Ps above needs to be explained with sources and industry standards.

Evaluating Competitive Dynamics

This segment will assist in the development of Section 4, "Strategic Positioning". When the word "dynamic" is used it is always important to note, dynamic means that it is an important, critical, and changing force that drives something. Dynamics can refer to everything including market dynamics, conflict mineral dynamics, political dynamics, and geography dynamics. The laws and regulations, as well as industry norms, can all be a part of what makes the innovation flexible enough to compete over a longer period of time. These are always large systems of influence that are ever-changing and affect everything.

Competitive dynamics then are the forces from outside of the organization that will create success or failure. For a business plan it is important that a minimum of five to seven research sources to be included in this analysis. To develop a portion of a business plan on competitive dynamics, consider this type of graph to help guide research:

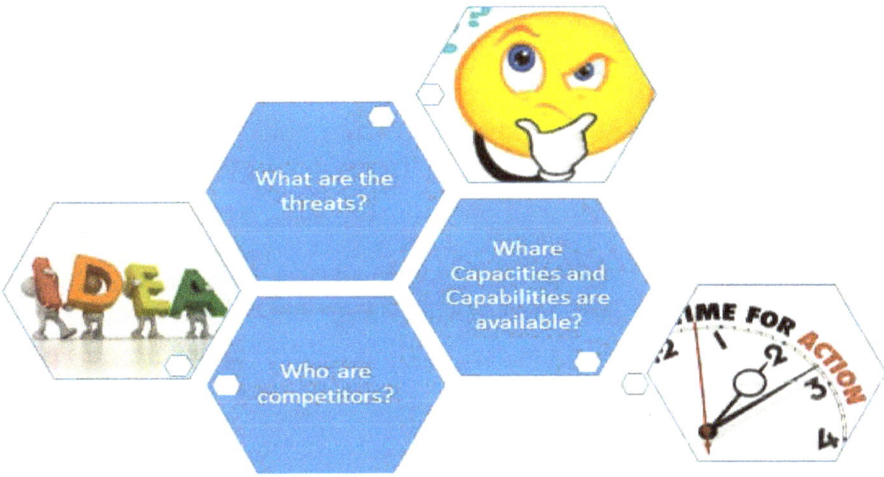

1. There is an idea, the innovation
2. What are the threats? What could go wrong inside the organization? What other opportunities will be passed up to accomplish this idea (opportunity cost)?
3. Who are the competitors (there are always at least three and up to ten)?
4. Does this system have the capacity, capability, money, time, talent, and motivation to make this happen?
5. Think through the innovation all over again from the beginning to end, considering more costs.

6. What is the action plan that is going to accomplish this?

Understanding & Targeting the Business Plan Audience

This will assist in the development of specifically the executive summary, however it impacts the entire business plan research, analysis, and writing. As with any communication tool (all documents and presentation are), it is important to consider the target audience for goods and service innovations. When walking into a Starbucks one can often see a particular "type" of customer (age, dress, level of spendable income, etc.). In fact, sometimes when people take a careful look, the majority of the customers at Starbucks are wearing the same colors (black and grey) and would have their dress code described as "business casual". Starbucks customers often do not want to wait more than five minutes for their order and will often walk out if the line is too long.

Conversely, when walking into a Wal-Mart store the people who are there shopping do not resemble exactly the types of people that can be seen at Starbucks. Wal-Mart customers often dress in brighter colors, mix-and-match outfits, are not as "business casual", often have uniforms or other more entry level jobs attire, not to mention the ones who dress barely at all, and finally customers with costume-like outfits. Wal-Mart patrons are often more resigned and will stand in a long line without too many complaints or even comments.

Another example is when going to McDonald's. There are usually young families with noisy rambunctious children, but when visiting a P. F. Chang's, there are usually couples who are a little more dressed up (more like the Starbucks crowd). And if families are eating at P. F. Chang's it is unusual to see an unruly or cranky kids.

There is no wrong or right to any of these groups of people. And neither is the consideration of the target audience as is not about judgement, but about identification and catering to the ways that the particular target audience would want to be reached. The words that are used on promotional materials, the colors, the font, and the method of delivering the advertising supplies are all specifically designed for the target audience.

This means that through research and data-driven decision making a particular, identifiable, and clear customer base has been identified and with that their traits, likes, dislikes, ability to spend, spending patterns, locations, preferred method of receiving information or meeting with others, etc. (CNN, Twitter, Facebook, etc.). There are a variety of ways to identify the target market and all of them take thorough research and in-depth analysis. This is a great article from Entrepreneur on how to identify a target market: https://www.entrepreneur.com/article/78002.

The most common target audiences for a business plan are:

- CEO of a company to fund or purchase the product or service or the idea of the innovation:
- The business plan needs to be data-driven, objective, and analytical; the CEO is most interested in the ROI over x-years.
- Financial institution to fund the innovation and business:
- The business plan needs to be data-driven, objective, and analytical; the financial institution is most interested in getting their loan and interest repaid on time. This includes the Small Business Administration (SBA) and can be found on www.sba.gov, it is a government entity that is designed to help fund small businesses.
- Venture Capitalist (VC):
- These individuals, usually with wealth, are looking to fund new businesses for a part of the ownership of the new business. Watching the business show "Shark Tank" on ABC will give an introduction to how VCs are working and thinking.
- Family and friends to fund the innovation and business:
- The business plan most likely needs to be passionate, interesting, and can be, in parts, subjective. Family and friends are more likely to invest even if they there is no significant ROI; they might be satisfied with just getting their investment back and not worry about interest or any payment beyond their investment; some might even donate money towards the new business.

With the above distinction of audiences in mind, it might become necessary for the business plan author to rewrite sections, if not the entire business plan, when considering a different audience. For example, if entrepreneurs are seeking funding from a financial institution and also a family member, two different versions of the business plan for the same innovation will be required.

Constructing the Management Plan

The “Management Plan” is Section 6 of the business plan. The management plan section of the business plan is one of the most misunderstood sections. Many students confuse management for leadership. One student unsuccessfully tried to “cut and paste” a section on Servant Leadership and make that a “management plan’. This student failed the section for two reasons:

1. It is plagiarism to cut and paste from previous work (even if it is the student’s own work)
2. A leadership plan is not a management plan

A management plan is not about theory; it is about action. An excellent management plan would include information on who, what, where, when, and how. It includes how to attract, develop, and retain personnel and a step-by-step analysis of who does what when. The management section always has job descriptions and these job descriptions connect to each and all of the steps to perform the innovation. For example, if a business plan is to open an internet gambling business then each of the following (and more) would be included in one or more of the job descriptions:

- Legal - risks, restrictions, regulations, and laws that apply
- Attracting - getting the right people to apply
- Developing - helping employees to do their job correctly; effectively, and efficiently
- Retaining - recognition and pay structures that keep employees engaged
- Organization chart - showing who reports to whom on what issues, with clear lines of authority
- Financial accountability - who performs the financial analyses, when, and who has proper oversight
- Marketing - who is responsible for each of the five Ps and who do they report to and who reports to them
- Operations - who is in charge of operations and who do they report to and specifically what steps will be taken to ensure that the products and or services will be delivered on budget and on time with sufficient quality

Note: In the twelve sections of the business plan there is a separate section for finance, marketing, and operations, but in the management section there are critical workflow and lines of reporting explained. Topics that will be covered later in the business plan can be mentioned and introduced earlier, but it has to be made clear that they will be addressed later on in detail and where they are located in the business plan (with section and page numbers given).

Creating the Operations Plan

The "Operations Plan" is Section 8 of the business plan. Operations is the process of how goods and services are purchased, produced, stored, packaged, transported, reach the intended user (or customer), how customer service is provided, and how the product or service is recycled. The operations or supply chain begins with raw materials and ends with recycling. One definition of operations is "the story of how goods and services flow through an organization". Operations topics included would therefore be process, flow, supply chain, suppliers, and all other parts of the operations that are committed to meeting the needs of customers while staying true to the mission and vision of the company.

These are a few, not all, of the key knowledge points in operations:

1. Understand strategy versus tactics and the relationship to product, service, and design
2. Recognize and demonstrate project management components and challenges from a global perspective
3. Communicate operations components, design, and supply chain management, which includes customer order fulfillment and Corporate Social Responsibility (CSR)
4. Summarize various quality control approaches and tools for problem solving and continuous process improvement
5. Identify technology for supporting operations management, collaboration, and innovation
6. Demonstrate effective written and virtual communication skills through the integration of Course Learning Outcomes in a course project or other learned pathways

These learning points are key as the operations plan is created. Remember, students may review their previous work from earlier classes, but cutting and pasting previous work is a failure of Academic Integrity and could cause students to fail the capstone.

In the operation plan the writer will demonstrate the step-by-step processes of how the product or service will pass through all life stages with details about sourcing, development, warehousing, shipping, and how the customer will receive the product or service. Additionally, operations often also include the total customer experience and call-centers for additional service and complaints. Operations also can be in control of the recycling or repurposing of the product or service. This is referred to as "Cradle-to-Cradle Operations" (Braungart, 2002).

The below graphics were created by Dr. Eckmann with SmartArt in order to demonstrate the concept of cradle-to-cradle operations in comparison to the often, in this context, misused production-to-distribution model. The first portraits the typical production-to-distribution model that is not cradle-to-cradle:

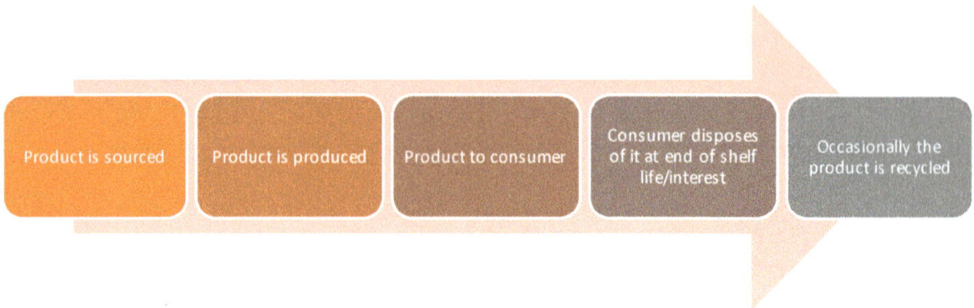

The second one, below, is the new, improved, and revised cradle-to-cradle production to distribution model:

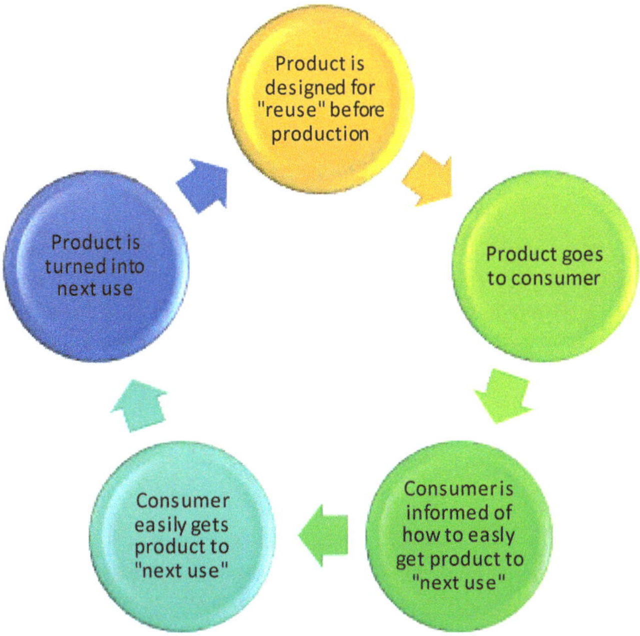

As the two models make clear, the evolution of the production-to-distribution is getting away from the arrow model to the circular type of cradle-to-cradle.

If a product is being developed and to be sourced or manufactured outside of the US, there are strong risks that need to be covered in the operations section. These include but are not limited to:

1. Often times manufacturing outside of the US costs more than inside the US. This is because travel for personnel and time lags need to be put into the hard costs of manufacturing outside of the US. Some sources claim that thirty percent needs to be added to the cost when manufacturing outside of the US.
2. The patent laws from the US do not cover manufacturing of products outside of the US. In other words, there is a strong risk that anything manufactured outside of the US will be copied without legal recourse as an option.
3. Transportation can be very slow, unreliable, and expensive. Consider if a product outsourced was to be shipped with this container company: http://www.zerohedge.com/news/2016-08-31/global-supply-chains-paralyzed-after-worlds-7th-largest-container-shipper-files-bank.
4. Tariffs and embargoes can occur or change quickly and have devastating consequences.

5. Political or geographic instability; think about what happened to many US manufacturers when the Tsunami in Japan hit and completely stopped the flow of many supply chains. See this interactive map below to track instabilities: http://www.globalincidentmap.com/.
6. Some customers prefer and will pay more for "Made in America"; consider the target market for the proposed innovation and consider if this might be the case.
7. Out of the country production cannot be controlled and often unwittingly companies get penalized or a bad reputation for violations of human rights and the environment for outside of US production can occur. Companies have gone bankrupt due to negative press that was not foreseen or anticipated.

It is rare that an innovation is purely a service (many are a combination of product and service). However, if a service and not a product is being offered as an innovation the clear steps of how the service fills a researched and viable need, will be described and cited. The details for the research, development, testing, implementation, and assessment will be clearly described with multiple resource citations on the industry, customer, and how the service will improve business.

Some business plans offer a service for a product delivering company. In that case details of the product and how the proposed service will improve the business will need to be clearly and completely described. For example, if the major players in the industry have no history of being open to mergers and acquisitions, proposing them such is probably not going to be accepted even if it makes financial sense. Another example is if the major players in the industry have no recent history of successful innovation and are still financially successful within the industry, there may not be an interest in innovation even if it creates a new revenue stream. Bottom line is, the innovation needs to show an addition in value for the industry and the major players within. An additional example, for some major players in a few industries "Made in America" is critical and for some industries prestige is more important than money. Prove the fit for the innovation and major players in the industry, not with opinions, but with detailed research and analysis. The operations plan is all of the "moving parts" of the business plan and explains all of the details of how the innovation "works and fits".

Remember to include:

- List of potential suppliers and rationale
- Production and service delivery procedures
- Supply chain process flow chart (how goods and services will flow from the supplier all the way through the organization to the customer). These are some examples: https://www.google.com/search?q=process+flow+chart&tbm=isch&tbo=u&source=univ&sa=X&ved=0ahUKEwiwj_qUwI3QAhXHh1QKHdwABsQQsAQISg&biw=1920&bih=97
- Overall Supplier Relationship Management (SRM) to include all ethical considerations
- Supply chain
- Logistics
- Packaging
- Transportation
- Physical plant layout
- Organizational chart for supply chain (if more than three people in operations)
- DMAIC – apply DMAIC in the operations section – demonstrate that it can be applied, not described, to the innovation
- Ethical considerations

A description of how the supply chain will be developed in order to create time to market, quality, innovation, or cost (it is impossible to build a supply chain to receive each of the four in equal measure as these are mutually exclusive (for example, time to market is more expensive).

Applying Value Chain Analysis

This will also be included in the operations plan. A value chain is defined by The Economic Times (2016) on their website http://economictimes.indiatimes.com/definition/value-chaina as, ". . . the whole series of activities that create and build value at every step. The total value delivered by the company is the sum total of the value built up all throughout the company." Michael Porter developed this concept in his 1980 book *Competitive Advantage*, a well-worth read.

Once the supply chain is created, analyze each intersection of the supply chain in order to determine the ways that they can maximize value. It is best to create a graph that highlights the findings, perhaps using SmartArt, for the supply chain (every business plan, just like every organization, has a unique supply chain). For example, supply chains can be built for innovation, cost, time to market, or HLE but it is impossible to have all four in the same measure and importance, one of these will take priority. Again, for business plan writers who are unfamiliar with building a SmartArt, view this instruction from Microsoft: https://support.office.com/en-us/article/Create-a-SmartArt-graphic-4c36e284-2b76-400d-99d7-6cf198a33a4b.

For example, this might provide a guide for a manufacturing supply chain:

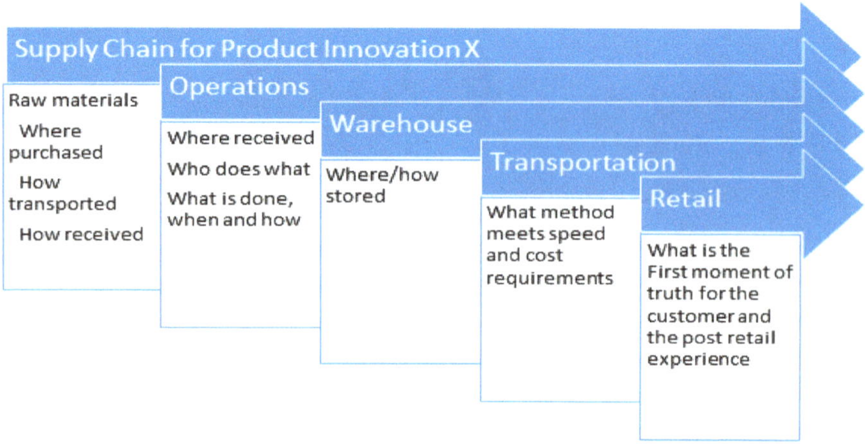

To prepare a value chain analysis use the above graph as an example, then at each point of the supply chain an analysis (with cited APA research) would demonstrate what is to be accomplished. This means that for raw materials to operations, operations to warehouse, or transportation to retail, a careful analysis would be performed that would determine the steps that will be used to create cost, time, and materials savings. This analysis would be completed using industry and supply chain research. This is an article from Harvard Business Review on how to create value at the post retail and customer experience: https://hbr.org/2006/05/winning-in-the-aftermarket.

The innovation is to prove that it will bring value to the marketplace and show how each step of the production of the product or service will be needed. Value is proven in the clarity of the explaination and details of salient research.

CHAPTER X - Implementation, Boards of Directors, & Concluding Thoughts

This part will assist in the development of Section 11 of the business plan. The financial viability of the business is critical for success. This cannot be stressed enough. The data in the business plan needs to be compelling to "win over" other options that the funding sources have for spending their money. Innovations for "good will" are not appropriate for most business plans. In fact, most CEOs will go to the financial section first, then read the rest of the business plan only if the financials present an excellent opportunity for growth and value. Most CEOs understand money, they may not be experts on marketing, operations, or even management, but most clearly appreciate and want a business plan to present a strong irrefutable case for additional financial gains.

The information learned or experience in working with statistics, economics, and finance will all be used as this section is developed. Remember, financial skills can be developed and learned. Some people will never be "great" at money, however help is available in many different ways. Templates can be downloaded from sites like Score.org and this site also gives thorough explanations and help on how to build a successful business plan. As mentioned before, there are many websites and books available that go into detail about the financial and other sections.

These are the main considerations for the financial section of the business plan:

1. Funding - Where will the money come from and why would they invest? Sometimes the innovation is offered as an idea or as a complete and finished product or service. This needs to be clearly stated and backed up with research.
2. Costs - What are the variable and fixed expenses? Costs for starting the innovation?
3. Profit and Loss Statements
4. Cash Flow Analysis

Remember there are templates for most of the financial data found on Score.org: https://www.score.org/resource/business-plan-template-startup-business. These are free templates, readily available and helpful, most students use them, but they cannot just "plug and play" with these templates.

Not all of the templates are appropriate for all innovations. So carefully examine the options and choose the ones that are fit for the proposed innovation. Each of the financial decisions needs to be clearly detailed and explained.

For some writers the financial section is the easiest part. For others, and most, this is the part that is dreaded. Check with others in the class, workplace, circle of friends, and family to find someone who has expertise in financials and ask them to review the work and offer to review their marketing section if that is the expertise. The writing partners can be of huge help in this section of the business plan. Learn from each other. That is what writing partners are for, to support each other and be on each other's side.

Remember, the financials from all of the Fortune 500 companies are readily available, to set context for the industry. View the critical financial data from the Fortune 500 companies in the industry and be sure that the financial section of the proposed business will meet the criteria and the emphasis areas for finance.

At a minimum these are the templates that are to be used for the financial section:

- Startup expenses
- 12-month Profit and Loss statement
- Break-even analysis

Simplicity is important in financials, however, key data needs to be clearly explained. Keep in mind, before and after each financial template a few paragraphs (or pages) of writing must explain the key points found in the numbers. It is not appropriate to just drop the financial templates into the business plan without clearly written explanations and foremost conclusions. It is highly recommended that the financials be included directly into the business plan and not put them at the end as appendices. This is due to the fact that the financial section needs to be explained as a critical and key piece of the business plan. Students need to follow these steps in accordance with the rubric for this and all other parts of the business plan.

Remember: Everything that is mentioned in marketing, operations, or management that has a cost attached to it needs to have a line item in the financials. CEOs and instructors notice if anything is missing. For example, if a promotion is mentioned in marketing and that cost for the development and the distribution of that promotion needs to have a line item in the financials. If key items are missing from financials that are mentioned in other sections, a business plan could be dropped a whole grade (from an A to a B) or the reader will dismiss the entire business plan as incomplete and incompetent from consideration.

Developing an Implementation or "Action Plan"

This part will assist in the development of Section 10, the "Action Plan". The purpose of a business plan is to create a step-by-step explanation of how to start a business based on an innovation and have it continue to operate successfully. At this stage and every stage of the business plan, the sections within must not be formed by opinion but must incorporate data-driven decision making. This means that all claims for funding, suppliers, industries, employees, manufacturing, design, and even customers must be substantiated by using business sources and academic journals (Harvard Business Review, Forbes, Bloomberg, New York Times, Wall Street Journal, Inc. etc.), as well as articles that are found in the Research Library. Each step of the business plan must be clearly grounded in research and analysis and cited using APA guidelines.

An essential part of the business plan is the action plan or the implementation plan. This is a step-by-step analysis of what is done when, how, and why. Most students put this in form of a graph or chart which is followed by data that supports why that step is taken at that time, how, by whom, and when repeated and who and when will perform all of the checks and balances. The action plan has a timeline so that anyone can look at the business plan and know what is done first, second, etc. The action plan may or may not look like the one below depending upon the innovation. However, it must contain at least this many action steps and will require that the what, when, by whom, and with whom sections are completed and all are cited. The action plan usually has at least thirty steps and many successful (funded) business plans have twice that many.

Once the chart is completed for the action plan, then another four or five pages will follow that will explain the details, stating the research completed to substantiate the order and categories. Also, this is NOT the financial section, this is the action plan that explains the steps. However, anything mentioned in the action plan must be fully explained and detailed, based upon research, in the financial section. A business plan often remains unfunded if there is no continuity across all parts of the business plan. In the business plan every part needs to be right. If there is any segment that is weak, then the whole business plan falls apart. A business plan is like a house, the walls, the floor, the roof, and the windows all have to work in sync with the other parts and if there are inconsistencies or weak parts, then the entire house (or the business plan) come undone, especially over time. To have a strong beginning or ending or a fantastic marketing section but a weak financial section, the business plan is not complete or sufficient; every section has to be rock-solid.

In other words, when a CEO (or an instructor) reviews a business plan, one of the first things they will review is that all of the items mentioned in financials are explained and detailed based upon research in the appropriate section. The CEO or funding source will always have others who are experts in the area (or several areas) review the business plan for viability, if they liked what they saw. This means that a person with marketing expertise will review the marketing section and a person with strong financial skills will review the financial section, and so on. With that, every part of the business plan needs to be strong.

To be specific, if the business plan mentions a marketing flyer in the marketing section, then the cost for that flyer (design, production, and distribution) must be detailed in the financial section. There must be a person who is responsible for creating and distributing the flyer and that responsibility would show up in their job description. Additionally, if the flyer is a major part of the marketing effort then the steps to design, create, and distribute that flyer would be in the action plan as well.

Date	What	When	By whom	With whom
Funding				
Connections with suppliers (listed)				
Initial marketing plan based upon demographics				

Initial operations plan based upon industry research				
Initial management plan based upon industry research				
Assembling Advisory Board				
Legal/Insurance issues research				
Hiring/Training				
Location research & selection				
Firming up marketing plan				
Firming up operations plan				
Firming up management plan				
Lease/purchase location				
Insurance and hiring practices with job descriptions finalized				
Begin hiring				
Begin training plan				
Purchase all necessary insurance/compliance requirements				

Set up regular Advisory Board meetings				
Analysis of first 30 days				
Reconsider if additional funding is required				
There are more... ***This is provided to get an Action Plan Started***				

Reviewing Internal Controls

This segment follows the previous section for obvious reasons. Once the action plan is researched and developed, a careful examination of all of the internal controls will be necessary. This can start with job descriptions and an organizational chart as these documents show who reports to who and what the job responsibilities are.

Every item that is mentioned in the marketing, management, and operations plans must be detailed and also assigned to someone in the organization to create internal controls. This is a great time to go back through the entire plan and see if there are clear lines of authority for all functions included. For example, if the student hires employees, then they need to pay unemployment insurance, taxes, etc. for all employees. In addition, someone in the organization needs to have the skills and the responsibilities that the innovation will meet all legal requirements.

Another example is that if the innovation has anything to do with food, then there are strict legal requirements. In some states food workers are required to have a food handler's license. Who in the organization will research this and who will be sure that they are in compliance? Another area that is often overlooked is Supplier Relationship Management (SRM). When a business contracts with a supplier (almost all suppliers have contracts), who will manage those contracts? What will be the terms and conditions for all of the suppliers? What steps will be taken to ensure they meet all of these terms and conditions? Who will monitor and communicate all discrepancies? If there are questions about SRM this very short article from Entrepreneur provides some great details: https://www.entrepreneur.com/article/206530.

Customer Relationship Management (CRM) is another area that will require internal controls. For example, what steps will be taken if the business has a high percentage of unsatisfied customers? How will the student or somebody else gather that information? When are existing complaints too many? Who will monitor the trends with customers? What will the parameters be for that person? Who will train them? How will they know when to go to the CEO with problems? This short paper from the Institute for Supply Management has specific details that will help: https://www.instituteforsupplymanagement.org/files/pubs/proceedings/dbawilliams.pdf. Additionally, the following video will provide more information on CRM: http://www.nimble.com/blog/5-must-see-ted-talks-to-improve-your-customer-support.

Considering a Board of Directors

There is an option to have a section on a Board of Directors for the innovation. This section needs to be carefully considered and included in the management section. If the innovation relies highly on marketing expertise it would be strong to have a member of the board (or two) who are marketing experts. If the business is to be opened in a particular location, it is often smart to consider having someone from the Chamber of Commerce from that city. Sometimes it is problematic to include too many friends or family members as often unresolved issues at "home" can cause a business environment to be less than productive. The Board of Directors needs to be chosen carefully to recap:

1. Choose someone who is interested in the success of the innovation; someone who will be "on the writer's team"
2. If the innovation is location-driven, then the Board of Directors might be chosen from an "insider" from the location of the innovation
3. If the innovation is marketing-driven, then the Board of Directors might consist of highly experienced marketing professionals
4. If the innovation is going to be financed by a funding source, then perhaps including someone respected by the funding source (if not the

funding source themselves); this is especially true for those who have experience or interest in the field of the proposed innovation

Remember, the Board of Directors is an advisory board. Choose individuals who can provide advice in the areas that the business plan creator will need the most help with. For example, if he or she is not strong in the financial analysis, advisors with strong experience and education in finance would be needed (but be sure they will be helpful and not just lecture; application is more important than theoretical knowledge).

Formulating Concluding Thoughts to Emphasize to the Reader

At the end of all sections of the business plan these were covered in "after-organizing paragraph" section. Concluding the business plan financial section is especially critical and will take more detail than the other sections. For financials it is imperative that there is a concluding section that gives all of the highlights of the financials because the financials are practically just numbers that are required to have meaning assigned to them.

The after-organizing paragraph for especially the financial section will carefully and succinctly summarize the financial value of the innovation and key opportunities for additional revenue streams. This will formulate what the numbers mean. This section or conclusions might be the only thing a busy CEO will read, so make it strong, clear, and have it include all of the highlights. Each of the financial templates that were used need to be highlighted, detailed, and explained so that the value the innovation will bring is abundantly clear. Specifically, the initial investment, cost of goods sold, the breakeven analysis, net profit, financial projections over a three-year period, and ROI.

Please do not bring up any concluding information on data that has not been included in the financial section. Furthermore, do not put data in the conclusion paragraphs, only recap and highlight the key points found in the financials.

CHAPTER XI - Putting the Business Plan Together

The business plan has been built in stages and now it is time to "put it all together". This is critical work and takes time, patience, and skills. The following check list will guide the writer through this process. The goal is that each of the steps below will be completed with care. For anyone who would like to print out the list to complete it, it can be found in the appendix section on page 182.

- ❑ All sections of the business plan have incorporated all of the provided feedback (by the instructor, writing partner, etc.) into the final paper. (The sections throughout the writing process should already have implemented the feedback, but now is the time to double-check.)
- ❑ Make appropriate corrections to the paper based upon writing partner's and other's feedback.
- ❑ Review the paper again and aim for zero mistakes.
- ❑ Return the favor by reviewing the writing partner's business plan and returning the paper with helpful comments (for students).
- ❑ Take a moment and consider "what is missing?". It may be that after the whole plan is put together that some realize that the marketing section is weak or the operations section is missing a connection to the marketing section. Read the paper from a "balcony" level and see what is missing, redundant, or overstated.
- ❑ Look at the paper and see if each section flows into the next; see that each paragraph flows into the next, and each sentence flows well to the next sentence.
- ❑ Be sure the textbooks and all other sources have been cited from the critical core requirement classes (if applicable), at minimum, marketing, operations, and management.
- ❑ The bibliographies for each of the single papers are incorporated into the one Reference section at the end of the paper (using APA which means that all of the sources will be in alphabetical order and are only listed once). A minimum of ten to fifteen references in the final paper.
- ❑ Write an advance organizing paragraph before each section heading. These should be four to five sentences that introduce the next section.
- ❑ Write an after-organizing/concluding paragraph after major sections and remember to not bring in any new thoughts, but be sure to stress the highlights of the section and briefly introduce what is coming next. (Remember, introducing and concluding written work is an excellent habit especially in business).

- ❑ The final business plan has a common theme and voice and does not appear to be separate papers that have been "stuck" together.
- ❑ Take out all of the pronouns (we, use them, I) as they are often confusing; no need to use third person "the writer" and yet with care most of the pronouns can be avoided.
- ❑ Review using "global search" that the whole document is in Times New Roman 12 and double spaced.
- ❑ Take out and replace all of the cliché (by the way, in the end, etc.) and contractions (can't, won't, don't, etc.)
- ❑ Think about the innovation and develop a brand by using color and creating a company logo.
- ❑ Create a color scheme for the business plan that connects with the innovation. For example, a "green company" may use green and a wave renewable energy system might be blue (a business plan should be visually appealing). To learn what colors mean you can check this Website: http://www.color-wheel-pro.com/color-meaning.html.
- ❑ The graphs and charts "match" in color and format as much as possible.

Note: The list above can be expanded by the business plan writer if other issues that deserve special attention before submitting a business plan are found.

Once each of the boxes above has been checked off, has been researched, and incorporated with care, the chances having a successful business plan have greatly increased. It is important to take care at the "end game" of projects in business. This is an ideal place to practice paying attention to the "end game".

Knowing & Highlighting Data for Each of the Twelve Steps of the Business Plan

It is always important to recall that business plans that are not based upon opinions "I think it is a good idea" are rarely funded (maybe by an unsuspecting and unsophisticated mother-in-law). Each of the twelve sections of the business plan will have evidence and citations that show research, analysis, and development. This means that each of the key points in each of the twelve sections will show that the recommendations and options for the innovation have been based upon data-driven decision making. Two examples are given below; the first is an acceptable citation of a statement of fact and the second is unacceptable as it does not display the use of evidence:

Good/acceptable: "According to Census.gov the population of Fresno, California in 2013 was 509,924."
Bad/unacceptable: "Fresno has about a half of a million people."

- In application this means that the marketing section would have a minimum of seven to ten references that explain and highlight data that supports:
- Demographics
- Developing a marketing plan analysis
- Evaluating competitive dynamics and competitive advantage
- Understanding and targeting the business plan audience

A sophisticated reader of a business plan will doubt the veracity and thus withhold funds from a business plan that does not show cited sources for all statements. It is especially bothersome for the reader of the business plan if accounts are masked as fact-based but fail to be supported by data and facts. It is a good rule to follow to ensure that all percentages and numbers are cited and therefore show that they were taken from solid data sources.

Emphasizing Key Opportunities

Once the majority of research and analyses have been completed and cited, it becomes clearer where the competitive advantage and other significant indicators for the innovation and business will be. The data will indicate information, for example about competition and trends, that will show areas for opportunities and possibilities. Once these opportunities have been identified it is critical that they be mentioned in the executive summary (briefly) and then highlighted in all appropriate sections throughout the business plan. There may need to be some adjustments to "Strategic Positioning" in Section 5 as well.

For example, if the data indicates that there is a new technology that will appeal to the young male millennial, that the new technology can be afforded by the millennial, and that this cutting edge technology will appeal to that target market. This dataset, with its evaluation, application, and citation will be found in the executive summary, company description, industry analysis and trends, strategic positioning, product description, marketing plan, operations plan, financial plan, action plan, and conclusions and recommendations section. Ensure that the information is presented in a variety of ways that fit individually into the different sections. This also entail visuals, lists, and tables. Do not just copy and paste sentences and verbiage throughout the parts of the business plan; repetition is very obvious to the reader and makes the writer look lazy, ignorant, and not appealing for executives to finance. This emphasis on key opportunities will influence the entire business plan. However, it is critical to be clear of this in the executive summary and products and services sections.

Showing Data-driven Decision Making to Mitigate Risk

Risk is a known or unknown, but identifiable factor that could put the new business in jeopardy. Risk can be internal (inside the business) and external (outside of the business). Risks internal to the organization are often more controllable and risks outside of the organization are often uncontrollable or at least harder to keep in check. It is also commonly agreed upon that certain risks are not controllable but still acceptable. Risks include hundreds of things from weather, over supply chains, to employees, and even funding sources. A great example of a risk that was known but considered acceptable was the building of a nuclear power plant in Fukushima, Japan, in closest proximity to the Pacific Ocean, as many others have been built. There is an obvious risk to this, but as he ocean water is used for cooling the nuclear power plants, the advantage therein makes the risk acceptable. However, when a large tsunami occurred in that region in 2011 due to an earthquake, the power plant became vastly dysfunctional and dangerous for that matter, and this created a worldwide shortage for some of the materials for computer parts that were manufactured in that part of Japan.

As it has been discussed, data-driven decision making is found at the intersection of research, analysis, and critical thinking which have all been covered in this book. As a reminder, research is current, business-oriented, and from a reliable source (most often from New York Times, Wall Street Journal, Harvard Business Review, Forbes, Bloomberg, and gov sources). Magazine sources like People Magazine, Wikipedia sources, and .com are most often not considered sound research sources. One company's website is usually not considered good source material as a company website holds data that is not necessarily true and is designed as marketing or promotional material. Analysis is reviewing many sources and finding a common theme or trend in the data; analysis is never based on just one source. Analysis requires thinking, specifically critical thinking, which is looking at both sides of the data, positive and negative, considering law suits as well as resolutions, and comparing one company to another or the industry as a whole.

When analyzing information to mitigate risk, consider all data sources and especially any contradictory data. The following check list is provided by Score.org for risk analysis. Consider each of these on how they might apply to the innovation and business. This is a list of potential risks, but there are many more:

1. Financial - funding, global, US, local financial concerns, etc.
2. Sourcing - scarce materials, water shortages, energy shortages, pollution, transportation, packaging, etc.
3. Competition - someone else makes a competing product or service, cheaper, faster, higher quality, etc.
4. Management - law suits, sexual harassment, etc.
5. Changes in laws or regulations
6. Environmental
7. Weather, global, etc.

It is suggested that a check list is created with all of the potential risks for the particular innovation as each innovation has an individualized risk pallet. Creating and presenting a similar check list to the one below that coverers all potential risks is advisable. Not including an obvious risk is a red flag for funding and might deter the funding executive. This means the more detailed the risks that are analyzed and covered, the better. An excellent risk assessment table can be found on the government website Ready.gov under this link: https://www.ready.gov/document/business-risk-assessment-table. The risk assessment list below can found at https://s3.amazonaws.com/mentoring.redesign/s3fs-public/1-Risk%20Assessment%20-%20JUL%202014%20-%20draft%20071714.pdf:

RISK ASSESSMENT

To plan for recovery, you must understand what risks threaten your organization and employees.

This assessment checklist helps you identify and rate these risks. You can then focus your mitigation efforts on risks with higher importance, determined by multiplying probability and impact (on a scale of 1 to 5, respectively, 5 being the highest). Use the blank rows to write in other threats specific to your organization. Note: you determine risks to your supply chain in a separate checklist, so focus only on threats to your business and employees.

	Importance			Comments
EXAMPLE: meteor strike to building Risk	Probability	1	5	No reasonable mitigation techniques. Ignore.
	Impact	5		
EXAMPLE: transformer hit by lightning; power out for one week	Probability	2	6	Install transfer switch to allow generator power
	Impact	3		
Power outage: consider whether your grid is a priority for utilities to restore quickly	Probability			
	Impact			
Lost access to building: due to pest infestation quarantine, crime scene, etc.	Probability			
	Impact			
Critical equip. failure: server, key file server, heat or A/C, vechicles, computers/printers manufacturing line equip.	Probability			
	Impact			
Phone/Internet outage: cut cable, phone company power loss, phone server down	Probability			
	Impact			
*Fire: wildfires, nearby building fires, elecrical, oven and chemical fires are possible sources	Probability			
	Impact			

*Tornado: and other high winds. Impact increased if building is not storm-proof	Probability			
	Impact			
*Flood: may represent regional flooding from coast or rivers, or pipe bursts/leaks	Probability			
	Impact			
*Hurricane/seasonal storms: Ice storms or blizzards represent similar risk for other regions	Probability			
	Impact			
*Earthquake: weigh supply chain effects, not just your own building	Probability			
	Impact			
Employee absenteeism: those with unique skills or special needs for family	Probability			
	Impact			
Mass absenteeism: pandemic or transportation strike/ outage are causes	Probability			
	Impact			
Explosion/Spill: heightened risk if near highway, railroad, airport, chemical plant	Probability			
	Impact			
Crime/Terrorism: communications and transport likely to cause secondary challenges	Probability			
	Impact			
Forced bank closing due to regional disaster: loss of funds	Probability			
	Impact			
	Probability			
	Impact			

Page 1 /PrepareCT.com

CHAPTER XII - Presenting the Business Plan

Entrepreneurs need to be prepared to give a "5-minute elevator" speech on their business plan. Below is information on the PowerPoint for the business plan. This means that they need to be able to give a 5-minute pitch speech about their innovation and the organization that the innovation will support. It is about promoting the most important and impressive features about the business and should excite the listener to wanting to know more (details). The purpose of creating this short business presentation is manifold:

1. Entrepreneurs need to have excellent skills in short presentations
2. This short presentation will be very helpful for entrepreneurs who, at this point or in the future, want to make their innovation actually happen; if the PowerPoint is not good, the business plan may never be read by funding sources
3. This short presentation can provide a quick review for interested employers for promotion or to interview for a new position
4. Most people enjoy creating something that is fun (remember, this is about something that is well known and was hand-crafted)
5. Students often view their classmates' presentations in a "live" synchronous environment and students often find that experience "the highlight of their capstone or even entire program" fun; students enjoy seeing the genius of their fellow students
6. The PowerPoint could be printed out and provided as a handout for funding sources

Things to remember about creating a good and interesting PowerPoint presentation:

1. Visually appealing - use branding colors for the innovation
2. Factual - cover the main points of each major section of the business plan
3. Easy to read - not too full of data or too sparse
   a. No more than five points per slide
   b. No more than fifty words per slide
4. The PowerPoint is a marketing collateral, so it only brings up innovation positives
5. Must have a reference page for all data that is referred to on the slides (visuals and text need to be cited and referenced there and where they are presented)

6. Less is more - leave room for those who are viewing the PowerPoint to "fill in the blanks"
7. Pictures and graphs that were developed for the business plan can be used (should be used) in the PowerPoint presentation

If more information is desired on how to create an interesting and powerful PowerPoint presentation, this is an excellent source: http://www.businessinsider.com/8-tips-for-great-powerpoint-presentations-2015-1.

Here are the main points on how to fashion a good and successful PowerPoint presentation:

Entrepreneurs mostly only have a small time window (often only five minutes) to show their PowerPoint presentation. This translates into:

- Not more than one minute per slide of presentation time (this does not include introduction and references as they are not presented in a speech)
- Do not read the PowerPoint - give additional information and assume that the audience can read; this is because people will either read the PowerPoint or listen to the presenter, not both; therefore, the PowerPoint should be brief and the words that are spoken ought to amplify the presentation.
- Do rehearse - as five minutes go by very quickly and the PowerPoint presentation will most likely not be completed well without timed practice sessions before the "go live" presentation; most people have little to no experience in short-speech presentations
- If entrepreneurs have the option to record their presentation, they can record the rehearsal efforts to "hear how they sound and act (gesture)" before they present; however, most entrepreneurs do not have an option of using the recording for their presentation (frankly the technology often goes wrong and it does not give the listener and speaker the "real time" practice that this project is intended to provide)
- Do leave time for questions
- If a presenter is an introvert, they can have a bit of an unexpected advantage over the extrovert: audiences are often times enticed when introverts speak as they habitually only do so when they

have something important to say; therefore, addressees will "lean in and listen" to introverts commonly more closely than to extroverts

See the PowerPoint in the Appendix section on page 177 on how to create and present a good business plan PowerPoint presentation.

CHAPTER XIII - Understanding Business Plan Applications

Now that entrepreneurs have completed the writing of a business plan, they should consider all the advantages that are coming their way:

1. They can speak to funding sources with confidence, even if financial data analysis was not previously their strong suit; they are now well versed to talk money
2. Start to look at all of the job opportunities that business and entrepreneurship carries qualification for: http://www.indeed.com/jobs?q=BBA&l=
3. A total understanding of the "wide view" of business has been accomplished; once writing a business plan has been accomplished, no job or department is seen anymore as an "island"; the interrelationship between the sections of business correlate to the sections of a business and once a business plan is completed the entirety of business is much more clear
4. Whether this innovation is successful or not, writing a second business plan will be much easier; people who have one good idea for an innovation will most likely have more great ideas and the fear and intimidation of making it a reality is lessened

Most people have no idea how hard and extensive a business plan is to create. Do not expect others who are not experts in business or entrepreneurship to understand all that has been accomplished. However, when contact is made with serious business women and men, they will be impressed.

CHAPTER XIV - Concluding Observations

Students, innovators, and entrepreneurs have now taken their spark of an idea and sculpted a business plan with both academic and professional key insights. This book offered encouragement and insights for women and men who had business ideas but lacked the confidence, experience, and/or knowledge on how to sculpt those rough ideas into elegant business plans. After reading this book and preparing a business plan, they have joined the ranks of some pretty impressive and successful business leaders like Musk, Gates, and Balmer, just to name a few.

As previously mentioned and this is important to remember, writing is an art and the business plan is based upon a creative idea and will therefore never be "perfect". Perfection, as much as beauty, lies in the eyes of the beholder, in this case the reader. With that in mind, all the author can do is make the business plan as strong as it can be based on the data-driven analyses and the perceived needs of the reader of the business plan. Any artist understands the challenges and difficulties of calling their work finished, as it never really is. Perfection is unattainable and there will come the point when it is necessary to draw the line and see it as complete, not perfect. No later than when the deadline is up it has to be called finished and it is time to move on.

When sculpting a business plan and working the marble block of the idea, the awareness of the possibility of overdoing it, needs to be present. Chiseling too much away can mean to overthink and underdo it and lose focus and even more so, perspective. The sculpture of the business plan requires to be understandable by the viewer/reader and the perspective is therefore from the outside in, not the inside out.

The book has created ways to take "Ideas to Action" and bridge the gap from "a good idea" to turning it into a vibrant business.

This is what it takes to become an Entrepreneur!

Prisoners:

Michalengelo reviewed blocks of marble not to see what he could "make out of them" but what needed to be removed so that the "essence" of the blocks could shine through.

The same is true for writing a successful business plan. It all starts with an idea and through analysis and data-driven decision making, the innovator develops a plan of the "essence" of the business. It is not so much about creating but shaping the idea into action by removing obstacles and highlighting the essence of that remarkable idea.

References

Bhasin, H. (2016). Difference between goods and services. Retrieved from http://www.marketing91.com/difference-between-goods-and-services/

Braungart, M. (2002). *Cradle to Cradle: Remaking the way we make things work.* New York, NY: North Point Press.

Digha Nikaya. (n.d.). The issue at hand. Retrieved from http://www.insightmeditationcenter.org/books-articles/the-issue-at-hand/en/34/

Drucker, P. F. (1999). *Management challenges for the 21st century.* New York, NY: Harper Collins.

Drucker, P. F., Hesselbein, F., Kuhl, J. S. (2015). *Peter Drucker's five most important questions: Enduring wisdom for today's leaders.* Hoboken, NJ: John Wiley & Sons, Inc.

Eckmann, H. (2012). Strategic intent. Retrieved from https://www.saddleback.edu/uploads/ewd/documents/Strategic%20Intentions.pdf

Heifetz, R. & Laurie, D. L. (1997). The work of leadership. Retrieved from https://hbr.org/2001/12/the-work-of-leadership

Heifetz, R. & Linsky, M. (2002). *Leadership on the Line: Staying alive through the dangers of leadership.* Boston, MA: Harvard School Publishing.

Heifitz, R. (1994). *Leadership without easy answers.* Cambridge, MA: Harvard University Press.

Holmes, O. W. (2006). Talk: Oliver Wendell Holmes Jr. Retrieved from https://en.wikiquote.org/wiki/Talk:Oliver_Wendell_Holmes_Jr.

Samuelson, W., & Marks, S. (2015). *Managerial Economics* (8th ed.). Hoboken, NJ: Wiley & Sons

Swink, M., Melnyk, S., Cooper, M., & Hartley, J. (2014). *Managing operations across the supply chain.* New York, NY: McGraw-Hill.

Appendix

Time-Outs – Filling the Creative Well

"Play is the most important element in discovering who you are. Play will lead you right into your deepest desires."
~ Keri Smith, *Living Out Loud: Activities to Fuel a Creative Life*

Another basic tool for creative exploration is the time-out (often referred to as Artist's Date). Julia Cameron, in the book, *Walking in This World: The Practical Art of Creativity,* suggests the Artist Date is "Grounded in a sense of adventure and autonomy, the Artist's Date is a once-weekly, hour-long solo expedition to explore something festive or interesting to your creative consciousness ... the Artist Date is assigned play."

The Time-Out is a way to replenish the creative well. As creatives, we need to continually look for inspiration. Cameron, in *The Artist's Way* says the time-out is a way of "opening yourself to insight, inspiration, guidance." She says in morning pages, we are "sending – notifying yourself and the universe of your dreams, dissatisfactions, hopes." On time-outs, we are receiving.

Time-outs are a way to honor yourself as a creative person. It is committing to time with a friend, your inner creative child. That inner creative child needs nourishing and nurturing; a weekly date allows you to reconnect with her.

I typically go to craft, art supply, and fabric stores. Wandering the aisles, I get lots of ideas. I learned to take a notebook with me to try out pens and jot down ideas. Another artist date I love is to surf the net. While it isn't "going out" it serves the purpose of spending time with my inner artist immersed in viewing art. I'm amazed at how inspired I am at the end of an hour. One of my favorite time-outs is a walk in the park with my camera.

What about going with a friend? It's just not the same thing. That's a play date with a friend, not with your inner creative self. For example, when I view art with others, like at a gallery or museum, I can't help but be influenced by their perspective. While this is helpful for other areas, that is not the purpose of filling your own creative well.

Time-outs, along with Morning Pages are habits that support your creative process and journey.

Time-Outs: Getting Started

Get out your calendar and find a time of the week where you can slip in one hour. I find Friday afternoons to be good; you are the judge of the best time for you.

Write in your calendar, with a colored pen!, your date time for the next 8 weeks. Give yourself the chance for this to become a habit.

Hold that time to be sacred ... a gift to yourself. You are on a creative journey and you deserve this.

Write a list of 8 places you'd like to visit. You can use the following list as thought-starters.

- Browse Art/Cra stores. Wander through an art store and touch new materials and see new ideas. You might want to take along a notebook for ideas to try later. Perhaps buy a sketchbook while you are there to take with you on subsequent ar ist's dates – the lack of lines is so refreshing, plus the pages handle colored pens and glued papers.
- Your city might have an Art Walk. This is typically the first Thursday (or whichever day) of the month. Art galleries remain open that night. It's a fun way to see what is going on in your local art community.
- Visit an Art Museum. There are probably several in your community or nearby. t's a nice way to spend a Sunday a ernoon.
- Visit a local children's toy store. In the front of the store, near the cash register, you'll find "impulse buys" like stickers, stick-on stars, funny pencils and pens, bubbles. Indulge. Give yourself a star for every day you do morning pages. Use the funny pen to write your morning pages.
- Go the theatre or a concert. The smaller the be er. Local community theatre is a great way to play and replenish the crea ve well.
- Listen to "new music" – music that you aren't accustomed to. Treat yourself to a new CD or borrow one from a friend or the library. Commit to listen to at least 30 minutes of it without distrac ons and no ce how you feel during and a er the music.
- Visit a boo store. Wander through sections that you normally don't venture into. Some bookstores have comfy chairs where you can browse books without buying them. Be sure to take along a notebook for ideas that emerge.
- Visit the library. Go onto Amazon.com and select a book you'd like to "test before purchase." Enjoy the book without the commitment of purchase. If you read it while at the library, take notes in your notebook.
- Take a cooking lesson. Visit a kitchenware store and take advantage of their lessons. Or perhaps your ocal community offers lessons. Learn how to cook food that you don't normally eat.
- Play with clay. Get some form of clay, like modeling clay, fimo clay, play dough, and spend time seeing what forms emerge. Do this outside where you can get messy! This is fun to do with music playing.
- Arrange flowers. Go to a flower shop and let yourself pick 6 – 12 flowers that draw your eye. Arrangement in a new way and enjoy!
- Browse the web. Google something like "collage" and visit the numerous websites of collage ar sts. I spend many of my artist's dates browsing artist websites. I copy some of the art to my computer where I have a document called Inspirational Art. This is really he pful when I'm in need of inspira on for a project. Beyond the art itself, I like blogs where people talk about their crea ve process.
- Visit a hobby store. See what new items are there since the last me you went.
- Visit a home repair store. What new ideas emerge?

Don't avoid these just because they are supposed to be fun! And please don't avoid them because you don't have time. Make the time … at least twice during this course.

Morning Pages: Clearing the Way

The best thoughts most often come in the morning after waking, while still in bed or while walking.
~ Leo Tolstoy

Julie Cameron, in her book *The Artist's Way*, describes morning pages as three pages of longhand writing, strictly stream-of-consciousness, which are done each morning. Stream-of-consciousness writing is very different from *journaling*, which calls for conscious thought on a particular topic. Morning pages are what one of my students call "morning dump"; Cameron says they could be called "*brain drain*, since that is one of their main functions." No topic in mind, just putting pen to paper, writing whatever. Think of them as stretching exercises. Just as a runner stretches before a run, creative people use morning pages to prepare the way for a creative day.

Why handwritten? Mark Bryan, co-author of *The Artist's Way at Work*, says, "Years of experience have taught us that the morning pages are best done by hand. Computers may be faster ... but computers tempt us to edit, to shape our feelings into "real" writing. Morning pages are intended to show us our unedited thoughts and feelings; they are supposed to be loose, messy, disorganized, disjointed, and flighty. It is out of this deliberate chaos – a positive form of *not knowing* – that order will spontaneously be born."

Morning pages are for anyone who is seeking that inner creative self, anyone who wishes to try to be more creative. Not just for artists or writers, it works well for business people, for leaders and managers, for team leaders and team members, for individual contributors who wish to try something new. Morning pages are for anyone. Morning pages are a primary tool for creative exploration.

Why do they work? Morning pages allow the Censor and other inner voices to have their voice. Better in these pages than when we are at the computer writing or at the easel painting. Better to allow the Censor to have his say before the team meeting where you want to try something new. The Censor is not speaking the truth, however her negative opinions are keeping you in doubt (that is her job!) Julia Cameron says, "The point is to stop taking the Censor as the voice of reason and learn to hear it for the blocking device that it is. Morning pages will help you to do this."

I've written morning pages for about 5 or 6 years. A long-time early morning journaler, I find morning pages (what I call MPs) to be cathartic, energizing, boring, repetitive, interesting, useful, helpful. They are not meant to be creative. I write a lot about creativity, and on occasion I get a creative idea to pursue. But mostly I make lists of things I need to do that day, I write about all the petty stuff that gets in the way of being creative, I just put pen to paper for 3 pages and move on. The more I write morning pages, the more useful they are for working out ideas and problems. On occasion, I'll write a letter to someone (you know, the kind of letter that is better not sent.)

Morning Pages: Getting started

If you want to try morning pages, don't go out and buy a fancy journal. Here is what you need to get started:

1. Purchase a spiral 8.5x11 notebook, college ruled. These are cheap and allow you to just write stuff and not worry about messing up a good artist's sketchbook or journal.
2. Select a spot for writing. I have a favorite writing chair. I keep my notebook and pens within easy reach. I sometimes write with colored pens, which I also have placed nearby. (A word on privacy. This notebook is for *your eyes only*. Do whatever it takes to keep prying eyes out of it.)
3. Select your time to write. It takes approximately 20 minutes to write 3 handwritten pages. It may take a little longer initially because your Censor may try to interrupt the flow of writing and you may find yourself editing what you are writing ... but as you get into this practice, you'll see there is no need for editing and the Censor can be happy because she has a place to be heard. It is best to do morning pages first thing. People who write and believe in mps get up a half hour earlier if necessary. I've had a practice since my children were small of getting up before them to have "my time." With my children grown and out on their own, early morning remains my most creative time.
4. Select a day to start. (Tomorrow is a great day!)
5. Write. 3 pages. Date it. Close the book. That's it.

To help you get started, here are some things to think about ...

- Write your first thought and keep writing your stream of consciousness... which is ANYTHING.
- Ask yourself, "How do I feel right now?"
- Call an "inside meeting" and visualize who is there.
- Ask, "Who wants to speak today?"
- Declare a day of the week for each of 7 Selves to share
- List all the things you need to do today and write about why you are doing them.
- Begin with "I wonder...."
- Write a letter to yourself or someone you care about.
- Write down a dream you had and write a story about it.
- Write about a problem or challenge you face at work. Brainstorm potential solutions; keep writing for three pages of ideas.

More Tips

- Set your intention and commit to what is realistic for you to feel successful.
- Do NOT use morning pages to beat yourself up.
- Honestly observe your PROCESS and learn.
- Create a "Sacred Space" for doing Morning Pages.
- Prepare the night before.
- Short ritual to get started and remember why.
- Find ways to add JOY to the experience.
- Music, candles, coffee, special pen

Business PowerPoint 101

Dr. Helen Eckmann
Brandman University
Heckmann@Brandman.edu

What and How to Make and Present a Business PowerPoint Presentation

Topics covered:

1. How to prepare a PowerPoint
   - What to include (plus a Handout)
   - What not to include
   - How long
2. How to present the PowerPoint
   - In Groups
   - Individually

Preparing a PowerPoint

1. Make an outline before you begin in a Word document (just for your own use)
2. Have 12 to 13 points (which will become slides)
3. Never have more than 70 words on a slide
4. Bullets are great – but not every slide
5. Stick with "normal" fonts
6. Be sure it can be read from the back of the room
7. Simple Graphs, Charts and pictures are good (but not every slide)

Preparing a Handout to go with your PowerPoint

1. Should be Marketing grade
2. Look like you would give to a customer
3. One page or tri-fold
4. Good design & attractive
5. Highlights the main points

What not to include

Any typos
Too many animations, fonts or colors
Everything you will be saying
Too much information

Please watch this
Short video:
http://www.youtube.com/watch?v=lpvgfmEU2Ck

How Long?

Ten to Fifteen slides is ideal
Anything over 20 is probably too long
Sometimes five is enough
Usually an odd number is good
The shorter the better – just key points!

How to Present a PowerPoint

In groups

1. Rehearse at least twice so you get the timing down (if you have a ten minute presentation and you have four people – you each get 1.5 to two minutes)
2. Be sure you never say what another member of your team has said even if it is on your slide
3. Never interrupt a team member
4. When they are presenting keep your eyes glued to them
5. Stand away from the Screen – each member different side
6. Never read your handouts – only take one 3x5 card with you with your notes
7. Talk to the audience – look at their faces
8. Do not ever read the slides in front of your audience

Individual PowerPoint Presentations

1. Rehearse
2. Get your timing down to the minute
3. Always answer any questions that are asked
4. Never read the PowerPoint
5. Take only one 3x5 card with you for notes
6. Ask questions of the audience like, "Did you know?"

Always recap at the end of your presentation

And leave time to do this...

- ❑ All sections of the business plan have incorporated all of the provided feedback (by the instructor, writing partner, etc.) into the final paper. (The sections throughout the writing process should already have implemented the feedback, but now is the time to double-check.)
- ❑ Make appropriate corrections to the paper based upon writing partner's and other's feedback.
- ❑ Review the paper again and aim for zero mistakes.
- ❑ Return the favor by reviewing the writing partner's business plan and returning the paper with helpful comments (for students).
- ❑ Take a moment and consider "what is missing?". It may be that after the whole plan is put together that some realize that the marketing section is weak or the operations section is missing a connection to the marketing section. Read the paper from a "balcony" level and see what is missing, redundant, or overstated.
- ❑ Look at the paper and see if each section flows into the next; see that each paragraph flows into the next, and each sentence flows well to the next sentence.
- ❑ Be sure the textbooks and all other sources have been cited from the critical core requirement classes (if applicable), at minimum, marketing, operations, and management.
- ❑ The bibliographies for each of the single papers are incorporated into the one Reference section at the end of the paper (using APA which means that all of the sources will be in alphabetical order and are only listed once). A minimum of ten to fifteen references in the final paper.
- ❑ Write an advance organizing paragraph before each section heading. These should be four to five sentences that introduce the next section.
- ❑ Write an after-organizing/concluding paragraph after major sections and remember to not bring in any new thoughts, but be sure to stress the highlights of the section and briefly introduce what is coming next. (Remember, introducing and concluding written work is an excellent habit especially in business).
- ❑ The final business plan has a common theme and voice and does not appear to be separate papers that have been "stuck" together.
- ❑ Take out all of the pronouns (we, use them, I) as they are often confusing; no need to use third person "the writer" and yet with care most of the pronouns can be avoided.
- ❑ Review using "global search" that the whole document is in Times New Roman 12 and double spaced.

- ❑ Take out and replace all of the cliché (by the way, in the end, etc.) and contractions (can't, won't, don't, etc.)
- ❑ Think about the innovation and develop a brand by using color and creating a company logo.
- ❑ Create a color scheme for the business plan that connects with the innovation. For example, a "green company" may use green and a wave renewable energy system might be blue (a business plan should be visually appealing). To learn what colors mean you can check this Website: http://www.color-wheel-pro.com/color-meaning.html.
- ❑ The graphs and charts "match" in color and format as much as possible.